A Gift For:

Nancy Grant

~~Betty Bonner~~

From:

Betty Bonner

Date:

2010

Published by J. Countryman® a division of Thomas Nelson, Inc., Nashville, Tennessee 37214
Managing editor: Jessica Inman

For a list of acknowledgments, see page 256.

Unless otherwise indicated, Scripture quotations are taken from
The Holy Bible, New Century Version, copyright © 1987, 1988, 1991
by Word Publishing, Dallas, Texas 75039. Used by permission.

www.jcountryman.com
www.thomasnelson.com

Designed by Thinkpen Design LLC, Springdale, Arkansas

ISBN 1404186530

Printed and bound in China

HO! HO! HO!

COUNTRYMAN
®

A Division of Thomas Nelson Publishers
Since 1798

www.thomasnelson.com

Contents

Introduction

SANTA GOT IT RIGHT

Christmas is the most wonderful time to—

• Catch up with friends and neighbors

• Savor scrumptious food and goodies without a scintilla of guilt

• Express generosity through gift giving and service to others

• Reconnect with family and celebrate family traditions

• Reaffirm faith by celebrating the birth of the Baby in the manger

• Follow the example of that jolly fellow from history and myth—and let out some loud, boisterous, from-the-gut "ho ho ho's!"

Maybe the Santa in the red suit with the reindeer, the toy factory, and the insatiable appetite for cookies and milk is more myth than fact, but he certainly got one thing right: Christmas is a time for laughter and joy!

The angels announced to shepherds: "Peace on earth, goodwill to men." And the fat man in red gave a hearty "Amen"—and *Ho! Ho! Ho!*

Family and Friends

No groaning, griping, or being an overall Grinch because the neighbors invited you to their house for eggnog and hard-as-brick fruitcake—it is the Christmas season, after all!

And think of the alternative. Who wants to be alone for the holidays?

Even if Aunt Mabel has more hair on her chin than Santa Claus, accept her invite, stop by, stay an hour longer than you planned, and enjoy the big bear hug and gristly kiss that await you!

Remember to welcome
strangers, because some
who have done this
have welcomed angels
without knowing it.

HEBREWS 13:2

Angel with an Accent

BEVERLY BUSH SMITH

Five days till Christmas, and the last thing I needed was a stranger in the house.

I'd abandoned my kitchen in chaos from a much-interrupted baking binge in order to dress for a neighbor's holiday party. Now, with one foot in my pantyhose, I answered the phone to hear a heavily accented male French voice asking for our son, Bryan, who'd lived in France for a year.

Bryan was out of town, not to be reached for two days, and I was beginning to think he'd invited *everyone* he met abroad to come visit us in Southern California.

There followed an exchange of fractured English (the Frenchman's) and fractured French (mine). Yes, he would like to stay with us. I hung up doubting my sanity. I'd now have another body in the house for Christmas, in addition to our two sons, their girlfriends, and my husband's parents.

But the day after the movie-star handsome, dark-haired Jacques arrived, I began to learn he was not simply another body, but a willing, able, and generous addition to the household. That afternoon, he asked, "You want that I prepare the crepes for dinner?" Did I ever.

He indicated he would make them both for the entrée and for dessert. I'd need only to fix a salad. Then he wrote this explanation for me: "Mattefin. It's the name of crepes of Alps."

He had a lovely touch with the delicate glorified pancakes, though the first two landed in the dish of George, our cat, as Jacques fine-tuned the heat of the stove. His special "invention," once each crepe was turned, was to break a single egg on top, stir it with a wooden spoon, then sprinkle a handful of Emmental cheese on top. He rolled the crepe just before the egg was completely set, producing a delectably moist creation, no sauce needed.

Jacques finished the dessert crepes with both orange-enhanced jam and chocolate sauce. Luscious.

The following day our visitor's next culinary offer produced "a dish of my region, Grenoble," a peasant dish, *pommes de terre gratin dauphinois.* Jacques thinly sliced potatoes to bake with milk, butter, bits of bacon, and plenty of Le Gruyère cheese.

Oven temperature was his only challenge. "They are still swimming," he reported, moving his hands in a pantomimed breast stroke before turning the heat higher. The hearty, savory potatoes were well worth the wait.

Jacques' talents extended beyond the kitchen. When I plugged in a string of Christmas tree lights and they failed to twinkle, Jacques assessed the situation with an "I fix." And it was done. When I struggled to create the centerpiece of Rome apples that looked so easy in the magazine, Jacques watched and suggested, "Maybe like this?" And he was right.

The day before Christmas, Jacques caught me as I began to assemble the ingredients for a baked Alaska. Did I "want that" he fix a *mousse au chocolat* for Christmas dinner? I noted that I'd already started the dessert.

"*Eh bien*, then we have two desserts."

Obviously, we didn't need two, and just as obviously, he was determined. I surrendered. And relaxed.

Christmas morning, as I cooked our traditional breakfast sausage and sliced my *stollen* coffee cake, Jacques appeared. "You want that I fix the eggs?"

"Fine," my husband answered. "Scrambled?"

Jacques scratched his head, frowning. *"Omelette?"*

I started to explain scrambled eggs and then decided, "Yes, omelet. Wonderful."

Later, Jacques used a dozen egg whites to make his glorious,

deeply chocolate mousse, then pondered the remaining yolks.
"You want that I make the mayonnaise?"

Homemade mayonnaise. What a luxurious dip for the veggies
before dinner.

At dinnertime, unsure if my standing rib roast had cooked
enough, I consulted the chef, who made a microscopic cut with the
tip of a boning knife.

"Off," he decreed over the oven knob.

"Not too rare?" I worried.

"Perfect," he pronounced.

And it was. So was the mayonnaise. And the mousse.

Marveling at how Jacques' presence enriched our Christmas
celebration, I hoped he'd stay—and stay.

But the morning after Christmas, his backpack stood by the front door.

"I have brushed my teeth," he explained in French, "so I can
smile my best to hitchhike to Tijuana, Mexico."

And so, with an embrace and a kiss on each cheek, he was
gone. I didn't know if Tijuana was ready for my French
guest/chef/decorator/cat nanny. But I did know that this
Christmas just wouldn't have been as fun without him. 🌲

Company's Coming

Sick of cooking for a party of fifteen? Thinking of punching your brother the next time he makes one of those comments about your job? Relax, take a deep breath, and remember some of the good things about having relatives in the house—

- You have someone else to blame for the lack of hot water after your shower.
- Where there are Christmas guests, there are very often cookies.
- Two words: hostess gifts. You need another key rack, don't you?
- Sleeping on an air mattress next to your cousin Josie—it's kind of like a slumber party, isn't it? All you need is a *Tiger Beat* magazine.
- The dog has lots of extra hands to feed him scraps at the dinner table.
- Your kindergarten nephew is the only one who has the guts to point out that last year Uncle Ron didn't have hair, but this year he does.
- With kids in the house, you have an excuse to keep a loop of Disney movies running on the TV.

And the best thing about having relatives around, of course, is that they fill the house with laughter and games and hugs and fun. So enjoy! And remember that you can still whip your brother on the basketball court.

*At Christmas play
and make good cheer,
for Christmas comes
but once a year.*

THOMAS TUSSER

The Christmas Tree

SARAH OLIVER

There were pine needles everywhere—on the couch, on the floor, down my shirt, and in my hair. Not to mention all over Richard's head, which was at the moment buried underneath the tree trying to figure out why it kept flopping over onto our couch instead of standing up in the tree stand.

We bought this cantankerous tree because it was Christmas—and not just any Christmas, but our first Christmas together. We weren't going to be at our apartment on Christmas morning, but I still felt like we needed a tree to get us in the spirit in the weeks before the big day. Plus, my parents have this great photo of my dad sawing the end off their first Christmas tree. He is beaming, smiling proudly at my mom, who is holding the camera. I always looked forward to having a similar moment with my husband on our first Christmas.

Two hours into our first Christmas tree moment, I am caught between the wall of our living room and a volatile pine tree. It could strike again at any moment, poking my face with its sharp needles while at the same time hurling several others onto our already littered carpet. That tree was fighting me, I was sure of it. One look at my shiny new Ikea furnishings and it wanted to bolt out the door. I was trying to hold it steady from behind while Richard sawed, twisted, and pushed, hoping to secure it into the tree stand. The tree refused to go in, insisting instead on throwing itself around the room and infuriating my husband.

I could have seen it coming. The way things had worked out for us so far should have lowered the bar on my expectations. But I am a stubborn idealist. I always have been. I expect the smiling husband in the photograph and everything that it suggests: a painless first attempt at Christmas, two completely different people coming together flawlessly, and a tree that practically walks into its tree stand and decorates itself in sheer delight at the privilege of being a Christmas tree.

I'd traveled to England to volunteer with a homeless project two and half years ago. Richard worked for the church that ran the project. We met my first day in the UK and haven't really looked back since. At the end of the summer, I returned to the States to finish my last year in college while he stayed in England to complete his master's. We talked every day, e-mailed, wrote letters, and visited every six weeks or so. It was better than a smiling photograph; it was a fairy tale.

He slipped an antique ring on my important finger a year later. We were going to ride off into the sunset, I was sure of it.

But the Department of Immigration and Naturalisation Services turned into the Office of Homeland Security after 9/11. It was an administrative nightmare of backlogged visa applications, new rules, and busy signals. On Christmas Eve the previous year, I sat in the guest room of my parents' house on the phone with my best friend as he told me that after months of research, preparation, and prayers, he had been denied a visa into the United States. He could not be guaranteed entry for our January wedding. We had been expecting to get married and live in America.

Four weeks later, I was boarding a one-way flight to England, dragging half of my belongings with me. The other half arrived shortly after with my family, who were coming over for the wedding.

The tree thing was partially my fault. This being my first Christmas in England, not to mention my first Christmas away from my family, I needed it to feel as much like home as possible. And, in light of the previous Christmas's major disappointment, I was determined to have the smiling photograph.

Of course I wanted to forge ahead on the new frontier of many Christmases to come in the Oliver household, create new traditions, be positive, and find exciting adventure in every hard situation—et cetera, et cetera—but when I saw several Christmas trees in pots at the local garden store, they did not look exciting or adventurous. Christmas trees in pots looked simply alien. Christmas trees go in stands with nice "skirts" to hide their unbecomingly knotty trunks. They sparkle and glow and touch the ceiling and take up the whole living room. Why would Richard want a small Christmas tree in a pot that barely comes up to his waist and needs to be put on a desk to look remotely substantial?

I'd forgotten he was English. I forget that a lot, considering that I live in England and hear his accent every day. I get frustrated when he comes up with strange phrases and ideas for how to do things and find it exasperating when he argues diplomatically. Aren't you supposed to wrestle through things with your gloves off?

In any case, he never forgets I am American. That's why we have this crazy Christmas tree throwing needles all over our flat: because he remembered that I am an American having my first English Christmas away from my family. He remembers that last Christmas I lost a lot of hopes and dreams, and he wants to make it feel as close to normal as possible.

He is definitely not smiling; in fact, he looks ready to throw the freakishly tall, unpotted Christmas tree out the window. I am not going to get my smiling photo, but I have something much better. I have a husband who loves me and who, for the past two hours, has been battling with a particularly rebellious tree just to make me feel at home this Christmas. 🌲

*Christmas greetings
speak of peace on earth—but
they don't say where.*

ANONYMOUS

Christmas at the Airport

PATRICIA LORENZ

My oldest daughter, Jeanne, hadn't been home for over sixteen months. A lot had happened to her in that time. In the spring, she'd been accepted to Yale University for graduate school in fine art. Her boyfriend, Canyon, graduated from nursing school, and in the fall, Jeanne and Canyon moved from California to New Haven, Connecticut, where Canyon got a job as an emergency room nurse and my daughter started classes at Yale.

Jeanne told me she wanted to come home for Christmas, but it was out of the question money-wise. Up to her eyelids in debt from her undergraduate studies, she was now facing even bigger college loans for her graduate work.

Shortly after Thanksgiving, I called my daughter with great news. "Jeanne, I can get you and Canyon friend passes from one of the pilots who stay at our house. Of course you'll have to fly standby."

"No problem, Mom! If we leave here on Saturday the twenty-first, we can beat the Christmas rush. Thank you so much! I can't wait!"

A few weeks later, Jeanne and Canyon arrived at the ticket counter at Midwest Express airlines at LaGuardia airport in New York at 5:30 A.M. after staying up all night to pack and leaving New Haven at 3:00 A.M. By some miracle, there were exactly two seats left on the plane after all the full-fare ticketed passengers were boarded. At 6:15 A.M. Jeanne and Canyon sauntered up the aisle of the DC-9 and slid into two side-by-side, extra-wide leather seats. Jeanne breathed a sigh of relief, knowing that in just two hours she'd be walking into my arms in Milwaukee.

"Jeanne Lorenz. Canyon Steinzig." Their names crackled on the intercom. As Jeanne fumbled for the flight attendant call button, a knot formed in her stomach. She raised her hand. "We're here," she said weakly.

The flight attendant walk up to their seats. "I'm sorry," she whispered. "You'll have to deplane. Two full-fare passengers just arrived at the gate. You'll have to give up your seats."

Jeanne knew the rules that went along with friend passes. No complaining. No arguing. Wear nice clothes. Don't make waves. Do what you're told. Smile and act like those friend passes are the best thing since warm chocolate chip cookies.

Jeanne and Canyon dragged their bags up the gangplank with a smile on their faces, but inside they felt like two thwarted pirates being forced to walk the plank. Jeanne knew it was four and a half hours before the next plane left for Milwaukee. *Oh, well—we can just take a long nap in the gate area*, she thought optimistically.

By 11:00 A.M. Jeanne and Canyon knew one thing: The person who designed those airport seats had never, ever, been stranded in an airport for hours after having had no sleep the night before. No matter what position they tried, the metal arm rests between each seat made it physically impossible to relax enough to even think of taking a nap. Instead of sleeping, they read and people-watched.

When final boarding was announced for the 11:30 flight and their names were not called, Jeanne felt a wave of nausea and hunger wash over her. The 3:55 P.M. flight was next—four and a half more hours of waiting. Because their finances were extremely tight, she and Canyon split a bag of M&M's and a grease-bomb cheeseburger for lunch. By 2 P.M. people-watching had lost its charm.

The airport swarmed with humanity that weekend before Christmas. It reminded Jeanne of what Ellis Island must have been like in the nineteenth century. She felt like a poor, tired, hungry refugee who was told to wait in another line for four more hours.

After the 3:55 flight left at 4:30 and nobody at the gate podium even glanced their way, even though Canyon had gone to the counter a number of times to make sure the airline personnel knew they were still waiting to get on, Jeanne contemplated getting on a bus and heading back to Connecticut. She paced. She sat. She watched. She fumed.

An hour later she lost it. "The heck with Christmas! This isn't worth it," she complained to Canyon. "Let's get out of here!"

He wasn't listening. Mr. "I can strike up a conversation with anybody" was chitchatting with a couple who had arrived early for the last flight of the day, the do-or-die 7:30 P.M. dinner flight.

An announcement came over the intercom, "Ladies and gentlemen, we're experiencing an overbooking situation and need volunteers to give up their seats until the flight tomorrow morning in exchange for a free ticket to any of the twenty-five cities Midwest Express serves."

The man Canyon was talking to suddenly excused himself and leap-frogged over people to get to the podium. "We can give you three seats," he said. "My wife, daughter, and I live in Manhattan and we can easily get back here tomorrow morning in exchange for free tickets." The gate agent thanked the man and proceeded to fill out his vouchers. Jeanne wanted to scream. There certainly wouldn't be any standbys on *that* flight.

Jeanne was ready for a fight. When the man returned, she glared at Canyon, wishing he'd stop talking to the couple and their twenty-year-old daughter. Jeanne was starving. Her head hurt, her back ached, her sinuses felt like they were ready to implode after breathing all that bad airport air, and she hadn't had any sleep for over thirty-six hours. She stood up and wondered if smoke was actually coming out of her ears.

That's when she heard Canyon say, "Why sure, we'd love to."

"Love to, what?" Jeanne asked bitterly.

"Mr. and Mrs. Caffrey have invited us to spend the night in their Manhattan apartment with them."

Jeanne glared at Canyon. Was he nuts? Stay with complete strangers in their apartment? In New York City? They could be serial killers, or drug dealers! She plopped down in the seat next to the couple who were still chatting with Canyon, dumbfounded that he would even consider such a thing.

Canyon had told them about his job at the hospital and about Jeanne's graduate work in art at Yale and learned that Mr. Caffrey was a psychologist and his daughter was a college student, studying art history. Jeanne was simply too tired to care and didn't offer much to the conversation. The man's wife, Esperanza, originally from Colombia, smiled a lot and spoke with a thick Spanish accent. All Jeanne wanted to do was sleep.

"We can take the bus back to Manhattan then catch a bite to eat at our favorite restaurant. You both could use a good night's sleep and a shower, I'm sure." Mr. Caffrey's offer was starting to sound like a dream come true. In a trance, Jeanne gathered her bags and blindly followed Canyon and the family out the door of the airport.

After insisting that they buy Jeanne and Canyon's dinner, Jeanne said her first prayer in days. *Oh thank You, God. Bless these people, whoever they are. And please don't let them mug us when we get to their apartment.* She knew they'd need what little cash they had to get back to the airport the next day and to buy breakfast and possibly lunch. They already knew the first flight the next morning was booked solid, but there was hope they'd make it on the second or third flight of the day. The longer they had to be at the airport eating that expensive snack bar food, the sooner their money would be gone.

When Jeanne and Canyon and the Caffreys arrived at the apartment, Canyon and Jeanne looked at each other nervously. The elevators doors opened and Esperanza said something to her husband in Spanish as she hurried down the hallway. In a moment they were ushered into their apartment just as the room lit up with hundreds of tiny white Christmas lights. A beautiful Christmas tree sparkled, as did the boughs of evergreen on the fireplace mantle. Standing there in the Caffreys' glorious home, decorated so beautifully in rich reds and greens, it suddenly felt like Christmas.

Mrs. Caffrey smiled and handed them clean sheets, pillows, and fresh towels. She showed them the kitchen, bath, and the rest of the apartment. "Please, please, make yourselves at home," she implored.

Mr. Caffrey spoke. "We'll be leaving early tomorrow morning. We're booked on the first flight to Milwaukee. You might as well sleep in and get to the airport for the 11:30 flight. Help yourself to food in the kitchen, and when you leave, just give the apartment key to the doorman." And with that, Mr. Caffrey shook their hands and went to bed.

Jeanne looked at Canyon, too stunned to speak. After a long, hot shower, she fell asleep before her eyelids closed on the Caffreys' comfortable living room sofa. The next morning Jeanne and Canyon ate a light breakfast, picked up the apartment, wrote the Caffreys an exuberant thank-you note, and left for the airport.

Even though they didn't get on any of the flights that day and had to spend the next night on the floor of the airport, they did make it to Milwaukee on the first flight Monday morning. Somehow, that whole next day and night at LaGuardia passed by not just in a blur of people-watching, reading, and talking, but mostly thinking about the Caffreys and their amazing gift of Christmas hospitality.

With all the travel madness, there was a chance that Jeanne would have been delivered to me irrecoverably cranky and exhausted. But the Caffreys' kindness gave her just the lift she needed to survive the mental gauntlet that is holiday airline travel. So I owe them a big thank you, which I shall dispense in the form of showing a little kindness of my own this holiday season. I'm staking out terminals as we speak.

Top Five Tips for Holiday Flying

1. Open "big" presents at home. Yes, it would be great to see little Suzy's face when she sees the six-foot Magical Princess Castle on Christmas morning at Grandma's, but no matter how hard you push, it ain't fitting in the overhead compartment!

2. Sit down with your family and review all calendars over Thanksgiving—that way, you can buy your tickets in advance and save money, and you don't end up with charge penalties when you belatedly discover your son got the part of Joseph in the church musical.

3. Head for the airport early and plan on there being extra delays and inconveniences—it's hard to feel the holiday spirit when you're stressed out and screaming at airport and airline personnel!

4. Take some small tokens of appreciation (gifts) along to give your flight attendants, gate agents, and pilots. It doesn't have to be expensive to get a huge smile of appreciation.

5. Dress comfortably *and* brightly—we can be so sophisticated that we miss out on receiving and spreading joy!

A good holiday is one
spent among people
whose notions of time
are vaguer than yours.

J.B. PRIESTLEY

Six Family Activity Ideas

These ideas work great for a group of good friends as well!

* Mixed Game Night. Combine shortened versions of Pictionary, Trivial Pursuit, Cranium, Monopoly, and other family favorites.

* Holiday Classic. Select a fun family movie like *It's a Wonderful Life*, *White Christmas*, *The Fourth Wise Man*, or *Miracle on 34th Street* to watch together.

* Lights of the City. Load up in the car and drive through neighborhoods and business areas that have great Christmas displays. Stop by a church that is hosting an outdoor "living nativity" scene.

* Great Neighbors. Work together to wrap up homemade treats or other small gifts to take to the neighbors. Have the whole family deliver them.

* Helping Hands. Volunteer as a family to help out in a soup kitchen or other outreach program for the needy. Discuss the joy of giving—not just receiving—during the holiday season.

* The Christmas Story. On Christmas Eve or Christmas morning, gather as a family to read Luke 2, the most complete biblical account of the Christmas story. Or select a classic from literature, like Henry Van Dyke's *The Other Wise Man* or even *The Polar Express*.

Gifts and Shopping

You don't have to break the bank to have a blast giving gifts over the holidays.

Set your budget, make a list of people to shop for—and go ahead and make it a long list—and find some creative ways to make what you've got go as far as you can.

Remember the boy who helped Jesus feed five thousand with his loaves and fishes? Throw in a healthy measure of faith and love to bless the people in your life.

*What I like about Christmas
is that you can make people
forget the past with the present.*

DON MARQUIS

Where Did Prince Charming Go?

LINDA RONDEAU

He opened his Christmas gifts first, and then, dancing with anticipation, he handed me my present. The gift bag was securely closed with a ridge of tape, evidence of his own hand in this artful presentation. I exercised all the pre-opening rituals: examining the glossy exterior at arm's length, carefully shaking it near my ear, and complimenting the packaging, as well as the obligatory, "Thank you, honey." I even ventured a few guesses.

"Jewelry?"

"No."

"Well, judging by the shape, it's probably not candy."

"You're right. It's not candy."

"Pajamas! Silk, right?"

"Nope. But you're getting closer. Go ahead, open it."

In an instant, I popped the row of tape and looked inside the satiny red wrapping bag. I froze in disbelief as I stared at what my husband had deemed the perfect gift.

A shower massage.

I was thoroughly convinced the romance in our marriage was more than dead. It was beyond resuscitation. In fact, it was stone cold. How could anything that required a crescent wrench to install possibly indicate otherwise?

I suppose it's only to be expected. After all, we've been married over twenty-five years. Can romance exist after fifty? Yes! Romance needn't die just because our hair had turned gray and our body dimensions had expanded. What did a utilitarian gift like this mean? Didn't he see me as attractive anymore?

"For me?" I feigned pleasure.

"Well, it's really for the both of us. That's why I spent a little extra."

I nodded. Since we bought a video camera as a mutual Christmas present to each other, we set a personal gift limit of $25. He went over the top to $30.

"You shouldn't have," I said honestly.

"I know you said you wanted jewelry. Surprised?"

"Oh, yes. I'm speechless, actually."

At some point over the past couple decades, the Prince Charming I married went through a metamorphosis, so much so that I dreaded the future. Could I really stand twenty-five more years of this? The handsome suitor who used to buy me Russell Stover chocolates had now emerged an aged athlete peddling Mr. Coffee. When had practicality replaced sentimentality? I wanted to find my delinquent fairy godmother and tell her to bring back Prince Charming.

Mr. Coffee was waiting for my reaction. I tried to infuse some enthusiasm into my, "Wow. Thank you, sweetheart."

"Pour yourself another cup of coffee and relax while I get it ready for you." He took the chrome monstrosity from the bag and, toolbox in tow, bounded up the steps like a schoolboy at recess.

The sounds of contented whistling could be heard downstairs while I stared into my coffee hoping to find some definition of middle-aged wedded bliss. I stewed in my disappointment. A shower massage. Humph! I felt like Grumpy, while Joe played the part of Happy.

"All set," he beamed. "You first! After all, it is your present."

"Yes. That it is." I trudged to the upstairs bathroom, took off my robe, and stepped under the wide tunnel of water. To my pleasant surprise, the steamy mist enveloped my senses. I felt as if I had just entered a sauna.

Well, now. This is nice. I took the showerhead in hand and experimented with the dial. Suddenly, reams of pulsating gushes hit my arthritic joints. I let my mind drift, imagining I was under a waterfall in Tahiti. It wasn't bad. Not bad at all.

Maybe he wasn't so far off the mark after all, I mused.

When there was no more hot water, I reluctantly turned the shower off, toweled dry, put on my bathrobe, and wandered downstairs.

Joe was anxiously awaiting the verdict. "Well?" He looked like an innocent child who had just given his mother a wilted dandelion, waiting for a hug of gratitude.

"It's out of the ball park, slugger. A grand slam homerun."

He smiled his cute little-boy smile. Behind his youthful grin, I saw the beam of love in his eyes, and found myself smiling back. I recognized the faded but familiar royalty with whom I fell in love with so many years ago.

Prince Charming still lived inside that paunchy but adorable man, I decided, and he knew exactly what this tired, achy body needed. 🌲

A Gift from Your Kitchen

HOT SPICED TEA

$1/2$ cup instant lemon tea

2 cups powdered orange drink

1 teaspoon cinnamon

1 teaspoon ground cloves

$2 1/2$ cups sugar

Mix all ingredients thoroughly and store in a tin, glass jar, or other decorative container. Tie with a ribbon and send home with guests who stop by your home during the holidays.

CHRISTMAS TRIVIA

Department stores see about 15 percent
of their annual sales in December;
jewelry stores about 25 percent.

Barbie's Letter to Santa

Dear Santa:

We've been working together, what, fifty plus years? During that time, I think you'll agree that I've been more than accommodating—I've greeted all your ideas for my career with a smile—and I'm sure our sales will reflect my trooper attitude.

That being the case, I hope you'll accept a few suggestions for improving sales and making the kids happy—and that's what really matters, right?

First of all, I'm not getting any younger, and I'm concerned about staying relevant. What do you think about some new career options? Doctor Barbie and Teacher Barbie were great in the 90s; how about something a little more cutting edge for the new millennium? I'm thinking Peace Corps Barbie and Socialite Barbie would achieve some level of hipness, as would, to a lesser extent, Fashion Editor Barbie or Publicist Barbie. Or what about Senator Barbie, CEO Barbie, or Grad Student Barbie? I think you see where I'm going with this.

In the same vein, I think we need to discuss some wardrobe

changes. In an effort to stay current, I've been watching a lot of MTV.
How do you feel about The Cure T-shirts and Converse sneakers?

Speaking of wardrobe, as I mentioned earlier, I'm not getting
any younger, and the heels have got to go. My arches are falling,
which, with all due respect, is at least partly exacerbated by the
fact that my knees don't work. Maybe we could discuss the new
joint technology at our next meeting. (Which reminds me: I feel I
should warn you about the possibility of a worker's comp suit filed
by He-Man—something about a repetitive motion injury.)

I'll be up north in late July—should I call Mrs. Claus to
schedule a brainstorming session? Maybe that would be a good
time to discuss stock options as well.

Yours always,
Barbie

As a little girl climbed onto Santa's lap,
the man in red asked the usual,
"And what would you like for Christmas,
little girl?" The girl stared at him,
open-mouthed, then gasped:
"Didn't you get my e-mail?"

The magi, as you know,
were wise men—wonderfully
wise men who brought gifts
to the Babe in the manger.
They invented the art of
giving Christmas presents.

O. HENRY

You Bet Your Boots

NANCY B. GIBBS

I glanced around and saw envy all over the other ladies' faces. It was the day after Christmas, and I was doing what women love most: shopping for shoes. And as spectacular as the bargains were that day, nobody noticed the markdowns nearly as much as they noticed me.

"What do you want for Christmas?" my husband, Roy, had asked me time after time between Thanksgiving and Christmas.

"I think I'd like to have a pair of boots," I mused casually a couple of times. He made a mental note of my request, and sometime before the big day, Roy went boot shopping. Unfortunately, he had no idea what size to buy, what color I would like, or even how high up my legs I wanted the boots to go. The poor guy was totally in the dark. He had no clue what I had in mind.

And so, when I opened one of my gifts on Christmas morning, I found a picture of a pair of boots that he cut out of a sale catalog.

"We're going boot shopping tomorrow!" Roy announced when I tossed the wrapping paper to the side. "Do you realize how many choices there are in boots?" he followed, a confused and somehow somber expression on his face. I smiled, imagining the look that must have crossed my sweetheart's face when he stepped into the women's shoe department and spied the wall of boots.

The next day, we began our mission to find the perfect boots. I figured Roy would drop me off in the women's shoe department while he made his way to the men's apparel—or to the other side of the mall to check out circular saws.

But, to my surprise and delight, when we walked into the boot department together, he asked, "Which ones do you like?" clearly not intending to go anywhere.

"I like these and I like those," I answered. "And these aren't bad." I picked up several other pairs as well.

"What size do you wear?" Roy asked.

"Seven and a half or eight," I replied.

Roy motioned for the sales clerk to come to the boot wall. "We'd like to try a seven and a half and an eight in this one," he requested. "And this one," he said, "and also this one."

Before long, the sales clerk came out with an armload of boot boxes. I dreaded trying all of them on—it's simply not as easy to reach my feet as it was when I was younger and more flexible.

I needn't have worried—that afternoon of shopping was time delightfully spent. Laden with boots, I sat down on one of the chairs, and then my sweet husband pulled up a stool and sat down in front of me. He untied my tennis shoes and took them off. He gently rubbed my ankles before placing the first pair of boots on my feet.

"Walk around and see how they feel." We went through the same routine through close to a dozen pairs of boots, laughing out loud and making jokes the whole time.

By the time we found the perfect pair, almost every woman in the shoe department was watching me with envious eyes. Not only did I walk away that day wearing the perfect pair of chocolate brown, mid-calf boots, I walked away arm-in-arm with the perfect man.

Did I feel special that day? You bet your boots I did.

*Christmas begins about the first
of December with an office party
and ends when you finally
realize what you spent, around
April fifteenth of the next year.*

P. J. O'ROURKE

You know you spent too much at Christmas when...

1. Your Visa bill is more than the equity on your house.
2. Your mail carrier starts wearing the leather Armani jacket you thought was for you.
3. Santa Claus complains that you're making him look like a cheapskate.
4. You lose one of your kids for two days under the mountain of presents and wrapping.
5. The CEO of Wal-Mart calls to thank you for helping the company hit its revenue projections for the quarter.

A Christmas shopper's complaint
is one of long-standing.

ANONYMOUS

How to Give a Spectacular Christmas Gift

BRUCE KARAS AS TOLD TO SUSAN KARAS

My wife, Sue, and I recently celebrated our twenty-eighth wedding anniversary. Over the years, we've had plenty of good times together, as well as our share of spats and disagreements. But we're pretty good about compromising when necessary.

Except, unfortunately, when it comes to Christmas shopping.

"What do you want for Christmas this year?" I'll ask hopefully.

"Surprise me," she'll answer—two words that strike fear in my heart.

"So…don't you want to know what I want?" I inquire next, thinking longingly of a particular fishing rod or DVD.

"Don't you worry about it—I've got a few ideas up my sleeve," she answers coyly with a peck on my cheek.

The conversation ends there. And there lies our problem.

I had clues right from the start that gift-giving would be a sore spot in our relationship. Sue could never comprehend my family's gift-giving habits at all. My family delights in asking, "What is it?"

before we open a gift, half expecting an answer. The element of surprise factors in very little in our shopping—and that drives Sue absolutely nuts.

"What's the fun of wrapping a gift if you all are going to pick it up, feel the weight, shake it, and then guess what it is before you open it?" She frowns and continues, "I can't understand it. Don't you like surprises?"

"Well, come on, Sue—your family's just as nuts. The way they go on and on about how much they love their gift—'Oh, a hundred thanks, it's just *perfect*.' A simple thank you is sufficient. Oh, and I don't need to know why they chose the gift or where they shopped for it."

"Well, fine," she says curtly, stomping out of the room.

"Fine," I answer, just to have the last word.

And so the Christmas gift rigmarole has gone through the years. Sometimes I start praying at Thanksgiving, *Lord, get us through the Yuletide season peacefully.* And sometimes we have. Other times, however, have been a disaster, with Sue in tears because I got her an electric mixer or a crock pot.

Women! Why do they want something romantic? Give them something they need, I always say. And then she gets mad because I don't surprise her.

Or, even worse, I don't like her surprise to me.

"You never like anything I get you! Doesn't matter what it is," she complains. But I can't help it if I don't like cashmere sweaters or fancy watches.

Why can't she just do it my way? It's so much easier. Just pick any item from my illustrated and annotated wish list. And please, provide the same for me, with size and color preference clearly denoted, thank you very much.

Then, one Christmas, some accidental eavesdropping on my part saved us.

I had come home early one day, unexpectedly, and walked in to hear my wife chatting on the phone. "No, I'm not even shopping for Bruce this year! I think I've finally learned. He wants something out of the West Marine catalog. He left the ad by the coffee pot.... Yeah, highlighted and everything. Not subtle at all. But that's okay; I can still go to the mall for my other gifts. I just decided to give him a gift he really wants this year."

I pumped a fist—I was getting my top-of-the-line Penn rod and reel.

My joy was short lived. Now I had to come up with a surprise for her—right? She was finally doing what I'd wanted all these years, and now I had to return the favor. How was I going to pull this off?

That night at dinner, I plied gently, "Honey, what do you want for Christmas this year?"

She handed me a Macy's ad. "I want this handbag."

She was going to do it my way this year?

"They go on sale this Sunday."

Even better! But, interestingly, rather than being thrilled to finally get to do Christmas shopping the way I wanted, I was suddenly touched by her change of heart. Now I was even more determined to give her the Christmas surprise of her life.

She interrupted my thoughts. "Hey, we've got be at Donna and Joe's by 8:00."

"Why? What's going on?"

"They're having a karaoke party." Her eyes sparkled.

Sue loves karaoke. And Donna and Joe have an awesome setup, complete with professional microphones and hundreds of songs to choose from. And they always put out a great spread too. Tonight would be great, as always—we'd kick back and enjoy an evening with friends. I'd worry about the gift dilemma later.

Everyone had fun visiting and laughing and, of course, singing. And in the spirit of *Star Search* and *American Idol*, we jokingly declared a tie between Joe's "Delilah" and Sue's rendition of "Crazy."

We left in high spirits, with hugs and "Happy holidays" to all.

That night, as Sue slept soundly and I lay awake with Journey songs ringing in my head, it hit me—the perfect gift, the perfect surprise. I slipped quietly out of bed and tiptoed into our den. I logged onto the Internet and began my search, and in no time flat, I was done. It would be delivered to a friend's house so Sue would never know.

The week before Christmas was a flurry of activity as all of us scrambled to get our last-minute shopping done and get the gifts wrapped and arranged under the tree. On Christmas Eve, we baked Christmas cookies and sang carols—and I slipped away to call my friend. He would drop Sue's gift off early Christmas morning on the way to his mom's place. I'd already wrapped the handbag she wanted, but it was only a decoy. All systems go on Operation: Surprise Sue.

When Christmas morning finally came, I was more anxious than a six-year-old. I couldn't wait to surprise my wife. We had a huge breakfast, then moved into the front room, where we sat around the glittering tree and opened our gifts amid the usual oohs and ahhs. Everyone was happy with their presents, especially me. I proudly held the oh-so-perfect rod and reel in casting position and shot Sue an appreciative smile. She held up her handbag and smiled right back.

Afterward, she looked around at the sea of discarded wrapping paper, bows, and ribbons. "Well, guess that's it. Merry Christmas, everyone! We'd better get this mess cleaned up."

"Not quite yet." I opened the door to the garage and lugged in a huge box. "One more gift here. For you, Sue." Funny, I suddenly felt nervous. What if she didn't like it?

Her eyes grew wide. "For me? Are you kidding?"

"Go on, open it!"

"Yeah, open it, Mom," the kids said in unison, in on my surprise.

She tore off the Santa paper and red ribbon and just stared in amazement. Then she almost cried. "My very own karaoke system, just like Donna and Joe's! Now we can host karaoke parties too, and I can practice any time I want."

I felt like I was on top of the world as I saw excitement and pleasure play across her face.

"Thanks, hon, this is the best gift you ever gave me!" She threw her arms around my neck and hugged me tight.

This was definitely the best Christmas we'd ever had—not because we both got what we wanted, but because we both learned a different way to give. 🌲

*The total value of shipments
for dolls, toys, and games
by manufacturers is
about $3.9 billion annually.*

*Once again we find ourselves enmeshed
in the Holiday Season, that very special time
of year when we join with our loved ones
in sharing centuries-old traditions such as trying
to find a parking space at the mall. We traditionally
do this in my family by driving around the parking lot
until we see a shopper emerge from the mall,
then we follow her, in very much the same spirit
as the Three Wise Men, who 2,000 years ago
followed a star, week after week, until it
led them to a parking space.*

DAVE BARRY

The Perfect Gift

LINDA RONDEAU

My brother looked at the belt he had purchased for my father. It was a perfect gift—our dad's old belt was frayed and ready to break.

He wanted it to be a surprise, but how does one wrap a belt? My brother's face brightened as he thought of a solution. He found five boxes that fit one into the other. He placed the belt into the smallest box, wrapped it, and then put the wrapped box into the next larger box, continuing the process until the belt lay in the belly of the largest box.

It took him nearly two hours to wrap the gift. Examining his labor, he was satisfied that the belt had been cleverly disguised. When Christmas morning arrived, he bubbled with excitement, pushing the brightly-papered box to my dad's chest and bouncing slightly on his tiptoes. "Hurry up and open my present, Dad!"

My father took the multi-boxed gift and shook it. "What could this be?" Before he could open the first box, my brother's exuberance spilled out. "You'd never know it was a belt, would you, Dad?"

Gifts for Her

(Sure to Get You in Trouble)

1. Waffle iron.

2. Bestselling diet book.

3. Subscription to *Car and Driver*.

4. Front-row tickets to Wrestle Mania XXIV.

5. *Sports Illustrated* swimsuit calendar.

6. Rudolph Christmas sweater that's two sizes too large.

7. Snow shovel.

8. Oil painting of your mother to go over the mantle.

9. CD with top ten truck stop Christmas classics.

10. Snow globe featuring your favorite football team.

11. Plunger, or anything for the bathroom that makes a funny noise.

12. Flintstones hand soap.

13. Gift certificate for facial waxing.

14. Pine-scented air freshener for her rearview mirror.

15. Extension cord—the big, orange, indoor/outdoor kind.

16. Ironing board.

17. Dictionary (unless she's a copy editor or it's a first edition).

18. The purse she already carries.

19. Socks.

20. The Clay Aiken bobble-head doll you got with purchase of a Big Gulp.

Christmas Angels

Christmas is indeed the season of giving. And one very special way to give is to give the gift of Christmas to a family who's hard on their luck. The Angel Tree is one charitable project that puts Christmas gifts in the hands of kids who have a parent in prison. You can find Angel Trees lots of places, like malls and churches. Or you can start your own tree by visiting www.angeltree.org.

Selfishness makes
Christmas a burden:
Love makes it a delight.

AUTHOR UNKNOWN

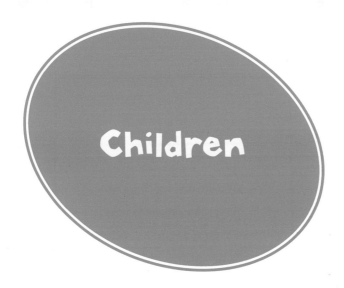

Children

Ever since a Babe was born in a manger, kids and Christmas just go together.

What do your kids want most for Christmas this year? You! Lavish the gift of time on them with board games, backyard football and chase, and stories.

No kids? Look around! Help buy gifts for the children of a young couple who can't afford much. Help out with kids' parties at your local school or church. And don't forget to act like a kid yourself.

Christmas is for children.
But it is for grown-ups too.
Even if it is a headache, a chore,
and nightmare, it is a period
of necessary defrosting of chill
and hide-bound hearts.

LENORA MATTINGLY WEBER

Christmas Cookies

Jo Haring

We have just finished making memories and building character.

As a short term gain we also netted a few sticky brownies and a much abused batch of Christmas cookies.

And I figure that those cookies and floured boys should be good for a few extra stars in my crown.

For my children, who generally concede me the kitchen chores through most of the year, demand as their Christmas due the making of Christmas cookies. And every expert who has ever addressed himself to the problem—Dr. Spock and Betty Crocker, to name a few—assures us that such an activity is a necessary part in the growth of healthy and well-adjusted children.

And that may be. But I consider it dangerous.

In flitting around the kitchen with small children you run certain risks—setting it and/or them on fire, or even worse, making a monumental mess.

And only those who have never had to clean up after a cookie-making child would consider the former worse than the latter.

Small children making cookies do not confine their activities to the kitchen. Their cooking results not only in cookies and an assortment of dirty cooking ware. It also produces dough-encrusted doorknobs, light switches, dogs, TV screens, drawer pulls, and sheets.

And there is no way a child can sift enough flour for a moderately large batch of cookies without producing a dust storm throughout the house.

There are a few rules that mothers of cookie-making children have evolved through trial, and mostly error, that would astound Murphy and pain Peter.

Rule 1: *If there are three children and four dozen cookie cutters, they will all fight over the Santa Claus cutter.*

Rule 2: *If you have three children and five rolling pins, they will all fight over the red rolling pin.*

Rule 3: *If you have three children and six bowls of dough, they will all fight over licking the bowl you have in your hand.*

Rule 4: *Anything that can be spilled will be; anything that can be stepped on will be; and anything that can be burned will be, including in addition to cookies and fingers, hot pads and tempers.*

But every Christmas, right after we have shipped off our letters to Santa, air freight, we dig out all the cookie cutters we can find and valiantly set out to make enough cookies to pass around the neighborhood.

For I am living, breathing, screaming proof that some people never learn.

It is an afternoon in which boy one dumps the eggs down the disposal, boy two spills the sparkles, boy three hits him, the dog cleans up the sparkles, and miraculously we arrive at the end of the day and the sugar at the same time, proudly displaying an ill assortment of exceedingly crunchy cookies.

And all three boys affirm happily that theirs are the best cookies they ever ate.

Then I cross off Christmas cookies from the list which includes Halloween costumes, Valentines, and Easter eggs.

I'm earning my old age a step at a time. 🌲

Never worry about the size
of your Christmas tree.
In the eyes of children,
they are all thirty feet tall.

LARRY WILDE

Rats

It was the Sunday before Christmas, and the children's department at church was putting on a wonderful performance.

Shepherds in bathrobes. Sheep in sheets and fluffy cotton costumes. Wise men with gold foil crowns. A baby doll wrapped up on blankets in a manger. Lines delivered with confidence, others with extreme, halting trepidation. The angel with a glistening silver halo.

To introduce a new song, a group of four boys were marched across the stage, each holding a large sign with one of the letters to spell out, "STAR."

The only problem was that in the confusion and choreographing the movements of almost a hundred kids, the director got them in the wrong order.

Afterwards, one of the parents declared that having his boy spell out the word "RATS" was the highlight of the show and most appropriate. 🌲

*I've learned that
I like my teacher
because she cries
when we sing
"Silent Night."*

CHILD, AGE SEVEN

Scrambled Christmas

DARLA SATTERFIELD DAVIS

"Deck the Halls with Bowls of Jelly!" Timmy skipped into the art room singing at the top of his lungs. "Good morning, Timmy." I said to the youngest of my first-grade artists. "Please take your seat and save the singing for the music room—or your shower," I said with a wink. The students all giggled and eventually found their seats.

"Today we are going to take a look at our artwork from yesterday entitled 'What is Christmas?' Timmy, since you are still standing and so excited, will you begin, please? Here's your paper, please tell us about your work." I wondered if even Timmy himself could decipher the explosion of color and figures scattered around his page.

And so began the most amazing Christmas story ever told. "Well, look here," Timmy began with enthusiasm. "This is where a big star was fallin' on some shepherds, and the angels were busy singing, so the guys on the camels had to come and save them."

The class looked confused, but Timmy gave them no time to comment or protest. "An' over here is where Santa Claus came down the chimbly and brought the baby Jesus to Mary who wanted one for Christmas real bad." Timmy looked up to make sure everyone could see his jumbled figures and bright splotches. "Mary cooked Joseph's goose for Christmas and they invited the Indians for dinner." My eyebrows shot up, but sheer curiosity kept me silent.

Timmy continued across the page pointing out the details as he went along. "The king didn't like the baby, so they put a tree in the window for cover, and deckerated it with stuff from Wal-Mart. And the star that fell went on the top of the tree! Rudolph and the red-nosed reindeers played some games and watched the baby Jesus, and a cow mooo-ved so she could see better. Everyone got presents, but Jesus got all the good stuff because He was the kid of the family!" Timmy stood with a big grin on his face waiting for the applause. The room broke out in chaos. Twenty-two children were all shouting different Christmas stories all at once trying to straighten Timmy out.

"Class, class!" I had to shout over them to get their attention. "Wait a minute."

Timmy looked crushed as he held his picture by one corner and let it fall to the floor. "Remember when we did the collages? When we took little parts of different pictures and glued them all together on one page to make a big picture?" They nodded remembering the fun we'd had. "Well, Timmy is so clever, he did the same thing with his painting of Christmas! He took parts of all the stories and put them together on one page!" I smiled at Timmy.

"Oh!" the class exclaimed. "Let us see it again! Come on, Timmy, hold it up higher!" they begged. Timmy happily complied and smiled over his shoulder at me as the other children pointed and discussed his work.

"What is the title?" asked one of the "accelerated students" who remembered we always try to name our special works. Without missing a beat, Timmy said proudly, "Scrambled Christmas!" 🌲

Twenty Ways to Be a Kid Again at Christmas

1. Go caroling in your neighborhood.

2. Go to the bookstore and read Christmas picture books in the children's section.

3. Build a snowman.

4. Throw snowballs at your neighbor's car.

5. Decorate sugar cookies—and be sure to make an absolute mess.

6. Go to the mall and see if you can buy five gifts with ten dollars.

7. Shake every box under the Christmas tree and guess what's in each.

8. Ask everyone you meet how many more days to Christmas.

9. Get your picture taken with Santa.

10. Put at least five marshmallows in your hot chocolate—the big ones.

11. Go sledding.

12. Watch a Christmas movie every night.

13. Get up at six A.M. on Christmas morning.

14. Leave cookies for Santa.

15. Go through a toy catalog and tear out things you'd like for Christmas.

16. Jump up and down with joy on your last day of work before the holidays.

17. Write a letter to Santa.

18. Shovel driveways and collect donations for the local homeless shelter.

19. Make a Christmas tree ornament—get creative with construction paper, pinecones, and glitter.

20. After Christmas, write thank-you notes, just like your mom used to make you do. Be sure to include lots of colorful stickers.

*The greatest gift that you can give
to others is the gift of unconditional
love and acceptance.*

BRIAN TRACY

The Purple Stocking

KAREN ROBBINS

I'm a traditionalist. No modern-art furniture for me—it's all about overstuffed sofas at my house. I love to cross-stitch and quilt. I make pot roast and mashed potatoes for Sunday dinners. And at Christmastime, I decorate with the basic Christmas colors: Christmas red and Christmas green. At least that's what I did before my mother asked my adopted six-year-old daughter what color stocking she wanted for her first Christmas with us.

My mother had knitted red and green stockings for our older three boys. Now that we had adopted Cheryl and her brother, Don, she was eager to begin theirs. Cheryl made her choice loud and clear—purple.

"Purple it is," my mother said, looking at me with her eyebrow raised to squelch my impending protest. The stocking had to be perfect as far as Cheryl was concerned, since this would be the first time in her six years that Santa might actually fill it.

She had hung stockings up in past years, but Santa had never come on that special night to put anything into them. The best Cheryl and five-year-old Don could expect to receive was a truck and a doll from their social services case worker. The gifts usually arrived a few days earlier or later than Christmas. The magic of Christmas Eve was never realized for them.

Anticipation and anxiety rose as Christmas neared. My twelve-year-old twins, Rob and Ron, and nine-year-old Andy could not comprehend that someone had never experienced the frenzied moments of sheer joy they knew as Christmas morning, tearing through layers of wrappings and boxes to find the treasures and desires of their young hearts.

Because Christmas fell on a Sunday, we decided to change our calendar and have "Christmas morning" on the twenty-fourth instead. That enabled me to enlist our neighborhood Santa in a surprise visit to our home on our Christmas Eve. That night, when Santa rang the doorbell, Cheryl flew to open it.

"Ho, ho, ho! So here you are," Santa exclaimed raising his arms in surprise. "I've been looking for you for a long time. But now that you have a 'forever home,' I know where you'll be."

"My stocking...it's purple...fireplace." Cheryl found it difficult to put a sentence together in Santa's presence.

"Well, make sure you go to sleep early tonight so I can bring Rudolph and the gang with my load of toys and fill that purple stocking with surprises," Santa chuckled.

"You're not landing on my roof are you, Santa?" my husband chided.

"Well, of course. Got to use the chimney. It's tradition, you know."

"Just who's going to clean up that mess the reindeer leave? I'm not." Bob folded his arms across his chest.

"I will! I will! I will!" Cheryl shouted, panic stricken that her new dad might dissuade Santa from making a return visit. Santa ho-ho-hoed and left after reassuring Cheryl that he knew the way back.

To my amazement, everyone cooperated at bedtime. Cheryl and Don were the first to be tucked in since they were the youngest. Andy soon followed, figuring that the sooner he got to bed, the sooner morning would come.

Our preteen twins, of course, held out to the last. Tradition called for Santa to decorate the tree on Christmas Eve. They stayed up long enough to see "Santa"—my husband and me—begin his work. But, not wanting to completely lose their Santa naïveté and become completely disillusioned just yet, they went to bed before it was done.

Our Christmas morning arrived early as usual. We had carefully outlined our family's Christmas morning traditions for our youngest and newest children, and when we entered the family room, we found all five children sitting side by side, the tree lights on. They were dutifully waiting for Mom and Dad to come down for breakfast, staring at the stockings now lined up at the base of the fireplace, heavy with goodies.

"He did come! He did!" Cheryl exclaimed when we appeared in the doorway. She jumped up and down and pointed to her purple stocking.

"So he did," I said, feeling a blush of the same excitement I remembered as a child. "Well, get into your stockings and then we'll have breakfast before we open the big gifts."

Cheryl cradled the purple stocking in her arms and joined the circle of siblings in opening the little candies, novelties, and fruit that "Santa" had stuffed in those precious knitted stockings.

After breakfast, Bob poured his traditional second cup of coffee to heighten the anticipation, but the kids nudged him into the family room before he could finish it so that they could open gifts.

We always take turns with our gifts so that each child can appreciate what he just opened, and so that Bob and I can savor each gleeful expression. After a few rounds, I noticed that the older boys were not busying themselves with their new presents the way they usually did, but rather sat awestruck by their new brother and sister. I noticed Ron brush a tear from his cheek. His face reddened.

"This really is the first Christmas for them, isn't it?" he remarked. I nodded and smiled.

I didn't get to follow all our traditions to the letter that Christmas—we went to Christmas Eve service at church on what was our Christmas evening, which deviates from tradition. And then there was the matter of the purple stocking, clashing somewhat with the red and green of my Christmas décor. But I'm open to new traditions, and each year, I hang that purple stocking right in the middle of the red and green ones. After all, according to tradition, the color purple indicates royalty, doesn't it? And isn't that what Christmas is all about—the birth of a King? 🌲

Christmas Groaners

*The way the holiday spirit makes you
feel like a kid again, you might actually
think these jokes are funny. Or not.*

* * *

Where do polar bears go to vote?
At the North Poll.

* * *

How do Chihuahuas say "Merry Christmas"?
Fleas Navidog.

* * *

What is green, covered with tinsel,
and goes "ribbit, ribbit"?
A mistle-toad.

A Christmas Prayer

Fred and Ted were spending the night at their grandparents' home. At bedtime, the two boys knelt by their beds to say their prayers. That's when young Ted began praying at the top of his lungs.

"I pray for a new ten-speed bicycle, a Death Star 64 system with Firestorm III and Death Match IV, lots of new computer games . . ."

Ted's brother, Fred, leaned over and nudged the younger brother. He asked, "Why are you shouting your prayers? God isn't deaf!" To which Ted replied, "No, but Grandma is!"

The Legend of St. Nicholas

Saint Nick, Father Christmas, Bonhomme Noel, Knecht Clobes. Who is the real Santa Claus?

In the fourth century, a young man named Nicholas was left a small fortune upon the death of his parents. He quickly gave away all his wealth to charity, particularly in ways that benefited children.

With his money gone, he became a monk. Though content to live in obscurity, his legend continued to grow, and he was appointed as the Bishop of Myra, Lucia.

Nicholas was eventually adopted as the patron saint of Russia. His day is celebrated in that country on December 6 of each year.

The exchanging of gifts, practiced in different ways around the world, is not only based on the gifts of the Magi, but also the legend of Nicholas's benevolence toward children.

Kids Rewrite Christmas Lyrics

- "On the first day of Christmas, my tulip gave to me"
- "Noel, Noel, Barney's the King of Israel"
- "Olive, the other reindeer"
- "Sleep in heavenly peas"
- "Good tidings we bring to you and your kid"
- "With the jelly toast proclaim"

*There's nothing sadder in this
world than to awake Christmas
morning and not be a child.*

ERMA BOMBECK

Santa Sighting

LANITA BRADLEY BOYD

"I'm staying up to see Santa this year!" I stoutly insisted, and my parents consented with surprisingly few objections. Nine years old and certain that I had the Santa thing figured out, I planned to catch my parents in the act this year.

My five-year-old brother, Larry, and I slept in an attic room only accessible by a drop-down stairway. We staged a Santa stakeout, making a pallet at the head of the stairs so we could peer down into the hallway that led to the living room. I talked Larry into lying there with me to watch, but of course he immediately fell asleep.

Soon, my own eyelids began to droop, only to spring open when I heard a noise at the front door—sleigh bells, unmistakably. Then I heard a stomping of boots, a thumping in the living room which had to be the sound of gift boxes being unloaded and stacked. I lay frozen with astonishment. As I carefully leaned forward to get a peek, I saw a large, white-haired, red-suited man, the classic Santa, standing there in my own living room. I stared, wide-eyed, as he took a step in my direction and gave a brief salute. "Merry Christmas, boys!" he chuckled, then turned and slipped out the door.

When I could no longer hear the sleigh bells, reason asserted itself, and I shot down the stairs and into my parents' bedroom, flipping the light switch and crying, "Aha! Where's Daddy?"

My sleepy-eyed dad rolled over, sat up, and said, "What's wrong? Why are you up?"

I stopped in shock. There under the covers were both my parents, asleep as usual. Then who was the red-suited man?

"You'd better get back to bed, young lady," he said. "You don't want to be up when Santa comes!"

"Oh, but he's already been here!" I cried, breathless. "I saw him! But he called us boys. You don't think he just left boy things, do you?"

"I don't know and at this point I don't care," Daddy said, uncharacteristically gruff. "I need my sleep!"

"Wait—" Mother sat up. "Did you actually see him, Lanita?"

"Yes! In the living room! And I heard his sleigh bells!" I answered, quivering with excitement.

"How wonderful!" Mother replied. "In all my childhood I never got to see him when he came. I always fell asleep. How exciting for you, darling!"

"Well, I guess it is," Dad grudgingly agreed. "But we still need to get some sleep. You'd better scurry back upstairs, Lanita. You can't look until morning."

So I went back up to my cozy pallet and snuggled up to my warm little brother, peacefully missing all the excitement. I trembled in awe at what I'd seen—and that it had not been my dad. Amazing!

When I was eighteen, I asked my mother who had come dressed as Santa that night. She gave me a blank stare. "What are you talking about?" she said. "It was the real Santa!"

And to this day, when I am sixty and she is eighty-two, she still gives me the same answer. 🌲

Nothing wrong with starting new traditions—especially once you're married and have kids of your own—but sometimes the best part of Christmas is doing things just like you did at Grandma and Grandpa's house.

If you never opened presents on Christmas Eve, don't start now. If you started every Christmas at church, load up the car and keep the tradition alive!

Better yet, reawaken a lost tradition from when you were a kid and start it with your family—like drinking eggnog while watching a favorite Christmas special. Anything that gets you and your loved ones together for laughter and fun is a perfect tradition.

And I do come home at Christmas.
We all do, or we all should.
We all come home, or ought
to come home, for a short
holiday—the longer, the better.

CHARLES DICKENS

The Christmas Spirit

MARK GILROY

I remember the first time my family stayed home for Christmas instead of traveling to Grandma's house in Detroit. I was seven years old. And I knew that it didn't feel right.

At Grandma's house there was always a real Christmas tree. At our house that year we had a dinky little silver tree.

At Grandma's house there was Uncle Ray, Aunt Esther, Aunt Naomi, and Uncle Dale to fawn over me. Actually, Uncle Dale did more roughhousing than fawning. But I liked that fine, even if Mom worried that I would get hurt—which I usually did.

At our house it was just my parents, my sisters, and me. We had great fun together. But that year something was missing.

There was no 180-mile drive from Dayton to Detroit; no 180 miles of bathroom breaks; asking if we were there yet; stopping for Coke (with more bathroom breaks to follow); playing "My Father Owns an Automobile"; singing and yelling until my dad couldn't take it anymore (somehow his eyes never left the road as he swatted my leg with pinpoint accuracy); and anticipating the bridge that made a funny noise on the car tires and made my stomach tingle when we crossed it.

At Grandma's house, there were tins filled with "million-dollar" fudge. There were cookies and other treats at our house, but no "million-dollar" fudge.

At Grandma's house, Grandpa was there. Not at our house.

When Grandma's house was sold, our family began gathering in Washington, D.C. But the house wasn't what really mattered. The traditions lived on: a neverending drive with neverending songs, a real Christmas tree, Monopoly and other board games (that never made us bored), "million-dollar" fudge, reading Luke 2 on Christmas morning, and of course, Grandma.

I can't remember another Christmas without Grandma until we started gathering every other year because of extended families. The years without Grandma still didn't seem quite right. And Christmas has never been quite the same since she died. The last time I saw her was on a Christmas Day. A few weeks later, the family gathered to cry, grieve, celebrate, laugh, and pay last respects. Grandma will always be remembered for her steadfast faith in the Lord and her love for her family.

And to this day, road trips always put me in the Christmas spirit. 🌲

Favorite Fireplace Christmas Readings

- The Christmas story from Luke 2
- *A Christmas Carol*
- "Twas the Night Before Christmas"
- *How the Grinch Stole Christmas*
- *The Polar Express*
- *Mr. Willoughby's Christmas Tree*
- *A Little House Christmas*
- *The Little Drummer Boy*
- "Yes, Virginia, There Is a Santa Claus"

Christmas Traditions
QUIZ

How well do you know your Christmas traditions? Here are seven
questions to test your knowledge of Yuletide traditions.

1. Which state is the top producer of Christmas trees?

    a. Pennsylvania

    b. California

    c. Oregon

    d. North Carolina

2. How long does a Christmas tree take to reach full growth?

    a. Fifteen to eighteen years

    b. Seven to ten years

    c. Two to five years

    d. Twelve to eighteen months

3. Which of these is not a character in *It's a Wonderful Life*?

    a. Janie Bailey

    b. Zuzu Bailey

    c. Harry Bailey

    d. Raymond Bailey

4. The word *wassail* means…

    a. A warm spiced drink

    b. A type of Christmas décor

    c. A Christmas tradition similar to caroling

    d. Both a and c

5. Which of the following has not recorded "Walking in a Winter Wonderland"?

    a. Michael Bolton

    b. Mandy Moore

    c. Perry Como

    d. The Eurythmics

6. True or false: The first electric Christmas lights were red, white, and blue.

7. Hormel's Cure 81 ham was introduced in what year?

    a. 1892

    b. 1922

    c. 1987

    d. 1963

Answers:
1. c. 2. b. 3. d 4. d. 5. a. 6. True. Edward Johnson, a colleague of Thomas Edison, was the first to display electric lights on a tree in his home. 7. d.

Next to a circus there ain't
nothing that packs up
and tears out faster
than the Christmas spirit.

FRANK MCKINNEY HUBBARD

Who Says Traditions Have to Make Sense?

JESSICA INMAN

When I was a kid, Christmases were all about my sister, who was five years older and my ally in Christmas fun. Together we baked cookies, shook gifts, and adorned the tree with ornaments we and our little brother made in school.

We also had our share of less-than-traditional traditions. For one thing, we made a game out of finding a stoplight pattern in the multicolored lights on our tree—red, yellow, green in a vertical formation. For another thing, we always hid a My Little Pony in the lower branches of the tree, straddling her plastic legs on a branch between the trunk and the needles.

And it wasn't just some randomly chosen My Little Pony. It was my Baby Surprise. (Each My Little Pony has a different hair color, name, and decorative stencilwork on her posterior which loosely corresponds to her name. Minty is light green with white hair and clovers; Surprise is white with chartreuse hair and purple balloons.

There's also a baby version of several of the Ponies—Baby Cotton Candy, Baby Surprise. Yeah, I don't get it either.)

My sister and I each had a Baby Surprise, and for some reason it was mine we hung in the tree. I think the story goes that her Baby Surprise was "good," while mine was ill mannered, and my Baby Surprise insisted on stalking the wrapped packages for some nefarious reason. I'm not sure why my Baby Surprise was the naughty one. I do know that she was much dirtier, despite the Wite-Out I used to try to restore her to her original color.

In any case, my Baby Surprise wanted to spend the holidays in the Christmas tree, guarding the presents or, more likely, trying to figure out what was in them. And because my mom thought it was funny, the tradition continued, and Baby Surprise even found her way to the tree during my high school Christmases. In fact, since we didn't exactly play with her anymore, my mom packed Baby Surprise away with the ornaments, and she reappeared each year along with the Rudolph I made out of clothespins in first grade.

Sadly, one Christmas shortly after I graduated from college, Baby Surprise met her untimely demise. Hidden within a thick blue spruce, she must have escaped our attention as we took down the ornaments, and the burning of the greens became her unfortunate funeral pyre.

And so Baby Surprise's neon yellow hair no longer graces the Inman family Christmas tree (which, by the way, now usually glows with white lights instead of colored ones at the insistence of my brother, thus putting the kibosh on the traffic-light game in addition to the Baby Surprise tradition—not that I'm bitter). I supposed she clashed with the burgundy frosted glass bulbs my mother bought a few years ago, anyway.

But I'm scheming. My sister's Baby Surprise, her curls still intact, her hooves pristine, may be called upon to perform tree duty.

She's such a goody-two-shoes, though, she'd probably start caroling or something. 🌲

Christmas Blues

You know you've got the Christmas blues when...

1. Santa doesn't leave you a present, but one of his reindeer does.
2. The eggnog in your fridge is actually half and half from last summer.
3. You go to your parents' house on Christmas Eve and discover they've moved—and forgot to tell you.
4. Your neighbors raise money to pay you *not* to go caroling this year.
5. Your cousin wraps and sends you the same gift you gave him last year.
6. Your letter to the North Pole gets returned with the stamp: "Address Unknown."
7. Your great-grandma declines your Christmas dinner invitation because she's on a Caribbean cruise.
8. The bell ringer outside the mall refuses your money but offers to leave you a few bucks for a warm meal.
9. The 10,000 lights your neighbor puts on his house shut down the power grid for your part of the country.
10. Since you started wearing that mistletoe hat, no one will stand closer than five feet from you.

Yes, Virginia, There Is a Santa Claus

We all have our favorite Christmas stories, tales, and legends, the ones we can recite practically word for word. One favorite holiday reading captures the essence of childlike in the response of an editor at *The New York Sun* to the following letter:

> *Dear Editor,*
>
> *I am eight years old. Some of my little friends say there is no Santa Claus. Papa says, "If you see it in the Sun it's so." Please tell me the truth, is there a Santa Claus?*
>
> *Virginia O'Hanlon*
> *115 West 95th Street*

He responded (excerpted):

> *Virginia, your little friends are wrong. They have been affected by the skepticism of a skeptical age. They do*

not believe except they see. They think that nothing can be which is not comprehensible by their little minds.

Yes, Virginia, there is a Santa Claus. He exists as certainly as love and generosity and devotion exist, and you know that they abound and give to your life its highest beauty and joy. Alas! How dreary would be the world if there were no Santa Claus! It would be as dreary as if there were no Virginias. There would be no childlike faith then, no poetry, no romance to make tolerable this existence. We should have no enjoyment, except in sense and sight. The eternal life with which childhood fills the world would be extinguished.

Not believe in Santa Claus! The most real things in the world are those that neither children nor men can see.

From a commercial point of view,
if Christmas did not exist
it would be necessary to invent it.

KATHARINE WHITEHORN

On the Tradition of Sending Christmas Cards

PAUL M. MILLER

For reasons probably known only to my neighborhood Gold Crown store, I assumed the yearly task of selecting and sending out the family Christmas cards. In actuality, "assumed" is not an entirely correct verb; the card responsibility was actually dumped on me because of my occasional snide remarks about how my wife was handling the task. In normal marriages, the wife of the institution handles things like Christmas cards, but because of my perfectionist spirit, it became my job by default.

I'm not complaining. I know I had it coming. I had an annoying way of asking questions and making pronouncements—

"You like that card?"

"No, we won't get imprinted cards—we need to sign every one of them by hand. It's more personal."

"Well, of course you should include a brief note. Just think of something to say."

"Now just tell me, how can one card design fit everybody on the list?"

In rereading the foregoing quotes, I have to admit that my attitude was a major reason that holiday card prep was foisted upon me. I must also admit that I have developed a philosophy for the yearly card prep and mailing process.

For example, has anyone done a study on whether card giving should reflect the sender or the receiver? What's the proper etiquette? I love ornate, stately, jewel-toned images, like stained glass windows, at Christmas; our friend Sara has a predilection for animals wearing clothes. So do I send her a card that reflects my love for all things Byzantine, or one with a Chihuahua in a Santa hat? Do you see my conundrum?

Now, another opportunity for obsessing about Christmas cards is that I often find it difficult to remember—

1. To whom we send a card.
2. To whom, under any circumstance, we don't send a card.
3. For whom we wait to see if we receive a card.

When taking over this job, I decided to redo our Christmas card and gift address list. That's when I found a handy spiral-bound book that has room for everybody's home and email addresses, phone numbers, and shoe size.

This same leatherette-covered volume also allows one to check off cards and gifts as they are received. Talk about a handy reference for point number three above.

I've noticed other holiday card decisions that are capable of causing tension and acid reflux disease. Such as:

- Even if it looks a bit like a "send me one too" hint, do we put a return address on our cards? And if so, does it go on the upper left hand corner (as preferred by U.S. Postal Service) or on the back flap (as preferred by the shy amongst us)?
- Do we hand-write our return address, or use those colorful stickers sent out by the likes of the Benevolent Society to Cure Diaper Rash? If we select the latter, do we make a contribution to the BSCDR's cause or throw away the return envelope and happily make use of the stickers anyway?
- What do we do with the cards that are left over after we've messed up addressing envelopes? There's usually an extra envelope or two in each box. But for those of us who have poor eye-hand coordination, one extra just isn't enough.

- Personal titles are another agony-producing consideration. While I probably won't send a card to the Pope, we do send our greetings to recent widows, divorced friends, the clergy, sons-in-law with newly earned academic doctorates, as well as friends with less nobly acquired advanced degrees. Can you understand the difficulty inscribing something as simple as a name on an envelope?

Much to my chagrin, even picking out stamps for Christmas cards can be dicey. When you ask the clerk at the post office for, say, a hundred stamps, he or she points to a display. The selection is really staggering. The following is only a partial list of the postage stamps offered at my post office offers during the season:

- U.S. flag (a good when-in-doubt selection)
- Looney Toons, Walt Disney, and Dr. Seuss characters (including Bugs, Mickey and Minnie, and Horton who hatched the egg)
- The "Love" stamp (ideal for wedding invitations and Dear John letters)
- Vegetables (I really did not see this one coming)

- Portraits of people who have done great things, but few of us have heard of
- Christmas/religious (a Renaissance Madonna and an out-of-proportion Christ Child)
- Christmas/secular (a cartoonish, vaguely manic Santa and reindeer)

All of these decisions are mere annoyances. My true holiday card pet peeve is receiving an envelope that has been addressed via a computer and printed on peel-off labels. Mass-mailed invitations to retirement seminars at Italian restaurants have gotten more personal than that.

And don't even get me started on Christmas family newsletters.

SEASON'S GREETINGS

Every Christmas, Americans send

1.9 billion greeting cards.

The Mystery of the Fruitcake

Jan Ledford

I never knew my husband's parents, but our first few Christmases as a couple, Jim constantly told me about his mother's annual fruitcake. When we had children, I decided to keep this Ledford tradition going by including it in our own holiday routine.

I'm not exactly a Betty Crocker type, so I spent hours surfing the Web and digging through cookbooks to find a recipe I thought I could handle. Eventually I located the perfect one and eagerly headed off to the grocery store. Soon the cart was full of candied fruits, nuts, and all the other ingredients. A week or two before Christmas I mixed it, poured it, baked it, and even aged it. And of course, I tasted and approved it.

At the end of January, I pitched it. The cake had "aged" beyond human consumption and still had only that one tiny bite missing that I'd sampled myself.

I was puzzled. "I thought your mom made a fruitcake every year," I said to Jim.

"Oh, she did," he affirmed innocently. "I never said we *ate* it."

Now we have a new holiday tradition: telling the story of the fruitcake that wasn't. 🌲

Merry Christmas to all,
And to all a good night!

CLEMENT CLARK MOORE

And to All a Good Night

Clement Clark Moore's "A Visit from St. Nicholas"—better known as "The Night before Christmas"—is undeniably a holiday classic. It's recited every year, sometimes in commercials and sometimes at kids' parties, and has spawned about a thousand parodies—"'Twas the Night before Finals" for college students, "A Redneck's Night before Christmas" for...well, you know.

It's such a sweet, happy tale that you'd think the poem originally flowed from the pen of a candy store owner, or . maybe a children's book author. But Clement Clark Moore wrote no other children's works and by all accounts did not own a candy store. A professor of classics at General Theological Seminary in New York, his most significant work before "A Visit from St. Nicholas" was *A Compendious Lexicon of the Hebrew Language*.

According to legend, Moore wrote the Christmas classic for his family during a sleigh ride (whether it was a one-horse open sleigh, we're not sure) in 1822, supposedly basing his oh-so-memorable description of St. Nick on the portly sleigh driver.

Moore never wrote for children again. In fact, reports have circulated that, being a stern, serious man, he refused to publish the poem, thinking it undignified. He didn't even acknowledge ownership of "A Visit from St. Nicholas" until fifteen years after a family member submitted it to a newspaper. He published it in a collection of his works, referring to the poem as "a mere trifle."

Ironically, that "trifle" is what made him famous.

Christmas Groaners

Warning: The following humor may cause pain. If you should happen to smile—you really are in the holiday spirit!

Q: What happens if you eat the Christmas decorations?
A: *You get tinsel-itus.*

* * *

Elf #1: What does Santa suffer from
if he gets stuck in a chimney?
Elf # 2: I don't know.
Elf # 1: Santa Claustrophobia.

* * *

Donner: How long does it take to burn a candle down?
Blitzen: About a wick.

No Place Like Home

Home Alone became an instant holiday classic, and will surely immortalize Macaulay Culkin, Joe Pesci, and Daniel Stern in the form of an annual airing of the movie around Thanksgiving. Most people who were between the ages of six and twenty when the movie released can quote the film all the way through. Here are ten lines from *Home Alone* that will in all likelihood "go down in history" (like George Washington).

- "It's not even rated 'R.' He's just being a jerk."
- "I made my family disappear!" (accompanied by wiggling blond eyebrows)
- "If it makes you feel any better, I forgot my reading glasses."

- "There's a lady calling from Paris. Sounds kind of hyper."
- "No toys, nothing but Peter, Kate, Buzz, Megan, Linny, and Jeff. And my aunt and my cousins. And if he has time, my Uncle Frank."
- "You guys give up, or you thirsty for more?"
- "Keep the change, you filthy animal."
- "Only a wimp would be hiding under the bed. And I can't be a wimp. I'm the man of the house."
- "A: I'm not that lucky. Two: We have smoke detectors. And D: We live on the most boring street in the United States of America, where nothing even remotely dangerous will ever happen. Period."
- "This is my house. I have to defend it."

Celebrations

From the company party to the neighborhood progressive dinner, the Christmas season is a time for celebrations.

But isn't that like trivializing the most intensely spiritual time of year?

Well, the angels did declare, "Joy to the world"—and the Babe who was born in the stable came to be known for enjoying parties and feasts. So enjoy! Celebrate the season.

*Did you ever notice that life
seems to follow certain patterns?
Like I noticed that every year
around this time, I hear
Christmas music.*

TOM SIMS

The Spirit of Christmas Past

GEORGIA RICHARDSON

The race is on. The sprint to be the first store offering fake Christmas trees, ornaments, candles, and lights has officially begun. Wasn't it just last week I was driving by yards with pumpkin-faced leaf bags full of the last summer's mow sitting by the curbs, witches dangling from trees along with ghosts wearing Mom's sheets?

Now, twinkling lights in red, green, and white have replaced the four-day-old orange and black of Halloween. Is it just me? I mean Christmas, last time I checked, was still celebrated near the end of December. You know, the twelfth month, the one following November, which is the month we give thanks for our families— and overeat. Any of this ringing a bell? (No pun intended.) So what happened? Can anyone explain when and why the start of the holiday changed?

To illustrate, I took my nephew to town the other day because we both needed coloring supplies—he needed colored pencils, and I needed hair...um...well, never mind. In each store, employees were clearing aisles and assembling "Six-Foot, Almost Like Real Christmas Trees," along with "1001 White, Twinkling, Rotating, Floating, Bubbling, Blinking, and Talking Light Bulbs." They had wreaths made of pinecones, berries, bows, fruit, and of course, six rows of the newest Christmas ornaments, plus stacks of candles in every shape, size, and color imaginable, including a certain infant King.

What they did not seem to have was school supplies.

Wasn't school still in session? Did someone forget to tell us that school was out because selling Christmas was in? As the next clerk came scurrying by carrying something giant and chocolate, I fell into step beside him and asked very quickly, "What the heck is that, and where are the school supplies?"

Never missing a beat, or even looking in my direction, he gestured over his left shoulder and said, "The 'To Die For' Santa and four aisles over, back corner."

So, after hastily making a mental note *(add one "To Die For" plus two Elvis candles to shopping list)*, off we went in search of the elusive school supplies. True to the clerk's directions and tucked away on the bottom, corner shelf were the remains of this entire town's school supplies. There were three spiral notebooks depicting some headless band on the cover, two packs of colored pencils, and erasers in the shape of every NASCAR racing team in existence. Later that evening, I recapped the day's events:

- The entire selection of school supplies: $12.15
- One three-foot-tall chocolate Santa: $21.99
- Half a dozen Elvis candles: $11.23
- One box of "make me red again" hair color: $8.79
- Forty-two, one-of-a-kind NASCAR erasers: $62.45
- The look on my nephew's face as we giggled, shared a pizza, and then broke off Santa's right arm for dessert: priceless

Well, maybe it is only November, and maybe it is a tad early to celebrate, but what the heck—'tis, evidently, the season.

Merry Christmas and happy new year to all—may your holidays be filled with laughter, your stockings with chocolate, and your dreams...well, may your dreams just be filled. 🎄

Ten Greatest Christmas Movies of All Time

1. *It's a Wonderful Life*

2. *A Charlie Brown Christmas*

3. *Home Alone*

4. *A Christmas Story*

5. *White Christmas*

6. *Miracle on 34th Street*

7. *Rudolph the Red-Nosed Reindeer*

8. *Frosty the Snowman*

9. *Christmas in Connecticut*

10. *A Muppet Christmas Carol*

Honorable Mentions: *The Grinch* and *Home Alone 2*

To: All employees

From: Management

Subject: Office conduct during the Christmas season

- Running aluminum foil through the paper shredder to make tinsel is prohibited.
- Playing "Jingle Bells" on the push-button phone system is forbidden (it runs up an incredible long distance bill).
- Work/vacation requests are not to be filed under "Bah humbug."
- The company cars are not to be used to go over the river and through the woods to Grandma's house.
- Do not use the workroom paper cutter or other company equipment to slice fruitcake.
- Do not use the color copier to print your family newsletter.
- Do not use the coffee machine to brew hot apple cider.
- Eggnog will not be dispensed in vending machines.
- In spite of the above, the staff is encouraged to have a Merry Christmas.

He'll Go Down in History

Rudolph the Red-Nosed Reindeer, popularized by a song performed by Gene Autry in 1949 and later in a 1964 TV special, has since become an icon in American Christmas folklore. Children everywhere sing "Rudolph the Red-Nosed Reindeer" every December.

But Rudolph was born several years before Gene Autry's tune hit the airwaves. In 1939, execs at the Montgomery Ward department chain recruited one of their copywriters, Robert L. May, to come up with an original children's Christmas story to be given away to customers as an illustrated booklet. May responded by creating a misfit reindeer who saves Christmas and earns a special "Ho! Ho! Ho!" from Santa himself. After rejecting other "r" names like Rollo and Reginald, May settled on a name for his lovable underdog: Rudolph.

Montgomery Ward retained the copyright to the increasingly clamored-for Rudolph story until 1947, when May, buried in medical bills incurred during his wife's terminal illness, persuaded the company to turn copyright over to him. After a commercial printing of the book and the release of a short Rudolph cartoon, May's brother-in-law, songwriter Johnny Marks, adapted the Christmas tale into a song.

Shortly thereafter, Gene Autry recorded "Rudolph the Red-Nosed Reindeer," selling 2 million copies the first year. The rest is Christmas history.

My Newlywed Christmas

JOAN CLAYTON

The first Christmas my husband and I spent as a married couple, we lived in "Vetville"—rows of Army barracks converted to apartments. All of our neighbors seemed to be in the same boat we were in: Going to school on the GI Bill and trying to make ends meet.

But we didn't know how little we had materially. We had each other, and being so much in love made us billionaires in our minds.

We searched and searched for a tree we could afford that first Christmas. We finally trudged home with our little three-dollar tree. We wrote love notes wrapped in shiny paper and hung them on our love tree. We thought our ornaments looked beautiful and vowed not to read them until Christmas Day. How well I remember one special note from my husband: "My darling, I love you more than life itself. You are the best wife I ever had." (I was and still am the only wife he ever had.)

To further demonstrate my domestic skills I secretly made him a pair of pajamas for Christmas. Someone had given me some hand-me-down material, and I worked on the pajamas all day while Emmitt was in class, then hid all the material, pins, and chalk under the bed before he came home. But I couldn't wait until Christmas. As soon as they were done, I gave him the pajamas early, urging him to open the gift and try on its contents.

As he pulled them out of the box and started putting them on, he looked awfully funny struggling to get into those pajamas. To his surprise and mine, I had sewn the legs together. I cried and cried.

Emmitt took me in his arms and said, "I didn't marry you because you make a mess of sewing." I cried some more.

Fifty years have come and gone since our first Christmas in the barracks. But I am still the best wife he ever had, even if I can't sew pajamas.

*Christmas waves a magic wand
over this world, and behold,
everything is softer
and more beautiful.*

NORMAN VINCENT PEALE

Eight Unusual Ho! Ho! Ho! Celebrations

1. Plan a special dinner and party for those served by a local mission or shelter.

2. Many people complain about not meeting new people and being lonely—plan a party where at least half the attendees are new friends.

3. Plan a neighborhood "kids" party, complete with games, treats, small presents, and a surprise visit from Santa.

4. Dress up like Mr. and Mrs. Claus and take presents to a local retirement home. You can take it one step further by putting antlers on the family dog and asking the staff if Rover can join you.

5. Work with your church to buy and send presents to a needy family or village in another part of the world. Make the shopping and gift-wrapping a family celebration.

6. If there's a hospice, convalescent home, or nursing home in your area, see if you can supply the cookies, icing, and decorations, and hold a cookie decorating contest for the residents.

7. Take a young couple out to dinner, and ask your kids to provide baby-sitting service if they have small children.

8. Host a dinner and gift exchange or a tour of Christmas lights for your church's college class. Throw in a hug or two, and you might just help a homesick freshman make it through finals.

Name That Tune

There are thousands of Christmas songs—we could never learn all the lyrics to all of them. (And some verses of some songs are popularly omitted for fairly obvious reasons.) See if you can match each Christmas song with its lesser-known lyrics.

1. SANTA CLAUS IS COMING TO TOWN
2. O COME, O COME, EMMANUEL
3. WE THREE KINGS
4. THE FIRST NOEL
5. JOLLY OLD ST. NICHOLAS
6. GO TELL IT ON THE MOUNTAIN

a. Myrrh is mine, its bitter perfume
Breathes a life of gathering gloom;
Sorrowing, sighing, bleeding, dying,
Sealed in the stone cold tomb.

b. Then did they know assuredly
Within that house the King did lie;
One entered it them for to see,
And found the Babe in poverty.

c. The kids in girl and boy land
Will have a jubilee
They're gonna build a toy land town
All around the Christmas tree

d. O come, Thou Key of David, come,
And open wide our heavenly home;
Make safe the way that leads on high,
And close the path to misery.

e. The shepherds feared and trembled,
When lo! above the earth,
Rang out the angels chorus
That hailed the Savior's birth

f. When the clock is striking twelve,
When I'm fast asleep,
Down the chimney broad and black,
With your pack you'll creep

Answers:
1. c. 2. d. 3. a. 4. b. 5. f. 6. e.

A happy childhood can't be cured.
Mine'll hang around my neck
like a rainbow, that's all,
instead of a noose.

HORTENSE CALISHER

A White Christmas

DIANE DEAN WHITE

The fifties was a time when so much was changing in our country. Many men had recently returned home from war, jobs were amply available with so many new frontiers and industries beginning to open, and new ideas were booming every day. I remember well our first television set. The screen was hardly more than a foot wide, but the wood that surrounded it was a beautiful polished oak. The only shows I recall were *I Love Lucy*, *Howdy Doody*, *The Lone Ranger*, and the shampoo and soap commercials.

The house where I grew up was a large, older home that sat on a street with a sorority house on one corner and a fraternity house on the other. We lived across from the main entrance to Michigan State College (now University). My parents rented rooms out to students, and we made lots of interesting friends from other states. The dividends were reaped in years to follow, as many of those students stayed in touch with Mom and Dad, visiting often and inviting them to their homes.

During the Christmas holiday we had the house to ourselves, as college was over and the guys who stayed with us went home to their own families. As soon as it was "just us" again, we went to the tree farm and cut down a Christmas tree, then took it home and got out our big box of decorations. The lights were the size of large colored eggs, and we always used silver tinsel and various homemade ornaments. Our durable star for the top of the tree made perennial appearances.

Once our tree-trimming work was done, we'd turn off the living room lights and step back to look at our beautiful Christmas tree. There were no gifts around the tree at that time; they usually appeared only a night or two before Christmas, so as not to tempt young eyes and hands curious as to their contents. For those few December weeks, my favorite time was early morning when it was still dark. I would creep downstairs to plug in the tree lights, then just sit next to the tree in my nightgown and robe watching the lights and enjoying the quiet with anticipation of what Santa would soon bring.

Every year, we made a trip to the city and a favorite department store and stood in line for a special visit with Santa. After telling him our hearts' desires, we'd get a candy cane from Santa's elf and return to Mother to share our talk with jolly old St. Nick. Christmas in the city was thrilling. There were streets of stores and red kettles with volunteers ringing bells to donate change to help others. Even the Planters peanut man appeared and would walk up and down the busy sidewalk with samples that drew people to the popular store with the wonderful smell. Clerks dressed up, many in bright bow ties, and there were a variety of special sales going on. Music filled the air at every store.

A memory I will never forget is the night we went to see the new movie *White Christmas*. We took the bus after Dad got home, and rode thirty minutes to the city. After looking at all the decorative window displays on the main street, we walked to the movie theater and watched the new release on the large screen. It hadn't snowed a lot that year, and Christmas was only a week away.

After Bing Crosby bid us farewell by crooning, "May your days be merry and bright, and may all your Christmases be white," we left the building happy, enthused, and enthralled. Blinking our eyes to adjust to the light outside the darkened theater, we were welcomed by the glitter and blessings of a fabulous winter wonderland. It must have snowed hard during the two-hour film, and with the excitement of the evening and now the beauty of the delicate white flakes, I knew I would never forget that magical scene.

A number of years have gone by since that time, and although many childhood memories are remembered with fondness, there is something special about that night and our family togetherness that has remained in my heart since. Whenever I see *White Christmas* on TV or hear the song, my mind goes back to a time when simple things were somehow the best of all.

It's a Boy-Girl Thing

According to the Alaska Department of Fish and Game, while both male and female reindeer grow antlers in the summer each year, male reindeer drop their antlers at the beginning of winter. Female reindeer retain their antlers till after they give birth in the spring.

According to every historical and artistic rendition depicting Santa's reindeer, they all have antlers. Therefore, every single one of them, from Rudolph to Blitzen, had to be a female. We should've known. Only women would be able to drag a fat man in a red velvet suit all around the world in one night and never get lost.

*The reason a dog has
so many friends
is because he wags
his tail instead
of his tongue.*

AUTHOR UNKNOWN

Rudolph's Sad Demise

TEENA M. STEWART

In addition to raising Maggie, a Newfoundland still in early puppyhood, my friend Patti was also raising young children. Ryan, her youngest, came home one day with a Christmas ornament made from a bone-shaped dog treat. The bone had been cleverly turned vertically to create a reindeer face. Ryan had glued on wiggle eyes and a little red pom-pom nose. Small pieces of brown felt and pipe cleaners served as ears and antlers, and a short piece of red yarn was glued to the back of the Rudolph's head for hanging purposes.

Ryan was so excited about his new ornament that he couldn't wait to hang it on the Christmas tree. But like most young children, Ryan was unable to reach too high. He stretched to hang the ornament at the edge of his reach, which barely surpassed the lowest branches of the tree.

A full-grown Newfoundland (or Newfie, as they are more affectionately called) can be the size of a small bear. They're affectionate, affable dogs who don't make much trouble, but their enormous size allows them to reach things that smaller dogs might miss. Sizing up Maggie—already tall enough to reach anything on the bottom third of the Christmas tree—Patti suggested they hang the ornament higher. She helped Ryan relocate Rudolph to a branch midway up the tree.

A surprisingly short while later, Ryan called to his mom. "Mom, my Rudolph ornament is missing. It's not on the tree."

"Of course it is," said Patti, walking over to the tree, but there was no ornament in sight. They looked under the tree thinking it might have fallen off, but they couldn't find it anywhere. "Surely Maggie couldn't have . . ." Patti mused, and as she looked over to the corner of the room, she spied Maggie contently licking her chops as if she had just finished up a tasty morsel.

"Oh, Maggie, you didn't," said Patti, walking over to the innocent-looking dog—a little too innocent-looking. Maggie gave her a big, slurpy kiss. Between her paws was one of the ornament's wiggle eyes and soggy pom-pom nose. Rudolph was long gone.

Lesson learned: Never hang a reindeer doggie treat ornament

within reach of a Newfie—or a Pomeranian or Portuguese water dog or any other breed, for that matter. Patti went out to the store that evening and purchased more bone-shaped treats. She and Ryan made a new ornament and hung it on the uppermost branches. This time Rudolph survived.

Christmas Groaners

These jokes are probably more likely to interrupt your celebrating with groans rather than laughs. But they might come in handy when it comes time to entertain your four-year-old nephew.

What do elves learn in school?
The elf-abet

What nationality is Santa Claus?
North Polish

If athletes get athlete's foot, what do astronauts get?
Missile-toe

Overheard on Fifth Avenue:
"Isn't it nice to see the Christmas
decorations going up?
Thanksgiving will soon be here!"

Love is, above all,

the gift of oneself.

JEAN ANOUILH

My Very Own Santa

KATHLEENE S. BAKER

My dad has always loved surprises, particularly at Christmastime. But last year, just when I thought he couldn't possibly have any more surprises up his sleeve, he managed to amaze me once again.

After my mom died, I didn't want Dad to spend the holiday alone at home. I was afraid that he would dwell on years past and that the holiday season would pass him by without offering him any joy or Christmas cheer. So my husband, Jerry, and I hosted my dad and Jerry's parents for "geriatric Christmas" gatherings at our house.

Talk about fun! Dad and my mother-in-law, Iva Dee, concocted an annual domino tournament during these visits. If Dad made a good play, Iva Dee would screech, "Raymond, I hate you!" Then they would giggle like little kids. Now and again we'd hear Dad holler, "Jerry, did you hear what your mother just said to me?" followed by more giggling and make-believe fussing.

I must confess that Jerry and I derived some entertainment from our parents' conversations. Let's just say that hearing aids are helpful, but far from perfect. Sometimes the questions and answers didn't apply to each other at all. The times they caught us snickering behind their backs, we would repeat the actual question and remind them of the discombobulated answer. They usually laughed harder than we did.

But last year, Dad broke the geriatric Christmas tradition by offering an invitation to come home for Christmas once again, just as I used to before Mother passed away. He even promised me it would snow in Kansas, which told me just how badly he wanted to host the celebration in his own home. We assured him we would be there. I prepared several dishes that would freeze for traveling and planned to cook side-by-side with Dad for the rest of the holiday feast.

A few days before Christmas, we loaded up our dogs, enough food for a month, and our brightly-wrapped gifts and headed north, the temperature dropping with each mile. I found myself getting excited even though it was going to be so different without Mother's presence.

As soon as we rounded the corner of Dad's street, my mouth

fell open. Under the deepening dusk, I could see that he had bought new outdoor decorations. We were greeted at the driveway by a herd of twinkling mechanical reindeer. I could not believe a man eighty-eight years of age would buy new outdoor décor, still climbing ladders to hang lights on the eaves of his house. The deer were beautiful and whimsical, but I was torn between cheering for him and scolding him about climbing ladders at his age, especially after his recent knee replacement.

But I didn't get a chance to scold him, because once we were inside, my mouth fell open again. In the living room stood a beautiful new six-foot Christmas tree, the ornaments spaced perfectly evenly. I wondered how many days he had worked at spacing those ornaments—I guess he knew that if they weren't perfect, I with my perfectionist tendencies would be puttering around with them all weekend. "Dad, your new tree is awesome! But what was wrong with your other one?" I was truly confused about why he'd bought a new tree.

"Oh, I never did like that other tree, and Mom always said we didn't need a new one at our ages." His eyes danced as he went on and on about every detail—looking at all the trees, finding the perfect one, and getting a bargain to boot.

There were more surprises in store. The dining room table was decked out with fine linen, a task I had assumed would be left for me. I commented on how nice it looked—and I didn't hide my surprise that he'd already dressed the table.

"Well, thanks," he said, sounding a little hurt, "but didn't you even notice my new candle holders?" I hadn't meant to hurt his feelings. He obviously wanted every single detail of this holiday to knock my socks off. I made a record-setting, split-second apology. I still don't know why he needed new ones, as there were several sets in the china cabinet. I guess it was just a year for extravagance.

Everywhere I looked, I saw a new decoration or an old favorite from years gone by. The whole house was a Christmas wonderland with every surface glittering and Christmas music playing in the background. I was amazed. How did he do all of this? How long did it take him? Even though he's still young at heart, he fights a terrible battle with arthritis in his back. Still, he had somehow managed to create a picture-perfect holiday happening.

We finally hauled our luggage to the guestroom only to discover electric candles in the windows and a floral Christmas arrangement atop the makeup stand. I caught myself smiling, wondering if there might be bright red sheets under the bedspread.

I was almost afraid to check the guest bathroom for fear he'd bought some of that lovely holiday print toilet paper. Fortunately, I found only more candles—the stores must have sold out of that cheerful tissue, or I'm sure he would have bought some just for kicks.

The desserts displayed in the kitchen reminded me of a Martha Stewart segment on TV. Dad had been cooking up a storm—there were cookies, cakes, and pies, all made from scratch, as well as several kinds of homemade candy. Christmas candles and holiday-print hand towels winked at us from every corner.

My head was spinning by the time I finished gawking around the house, but there was one more surprise in store. When the dogs started begging to go outside, I opened the back door and squinted in the bright, unexpected light. Dad had decorated the deck, looping and draping strands of flickering lights around the railings. "Oh my gosh, Dad! You've never decorated the back of your house. Have you lost your mind, or what?" I asked with a laugh.

I've never seen such a smug look on anyone's face in my entire life. "Well, I figured the doggies would enjoy it when they went outside." His eyes were sparkling much like the glittering lights around us.

The next day, friends and neighbors began dropping by to visit. Without fail, each asked what I thought of Dad's preparations, and each reported he had been on a mission to surprise the dickens out of me. It seemed nearly everyone in town knew what he'd been up to. And yes, I was most definitely surprised.

Just as when I was a child, this now-older Santa had made Christmas as special as possible for his now-older little girl. Never in my life had I felt Santa's love quite so deeply. 🌲

Welcome to My Home

There are all kinds of ways to make your family and friends feel welcome from the moment they step into your home—

- Spicy candles and potpourri
- Homemade baked goodies ready to serve
- A CD player loaded with Christmas music—oldies, goodies, and new favorites
- Candles, candles everywhere, along with twinkling lights to add sparkle on tables, countertops, bathroom shelves, and anywhere else that's safe
- A fire—real or otherwise—in the fireplace
- A small gift to warm the heart of all who enter your home

Around
the World

The angels declared "peace on earth and good will to all men." The Christmas season is a wonderful time to embrace the dynamics of compassion, forgiveness, and active love.

As you enjoy the traditions of other lands and say a prayer for those less fortunate, don't forget that "peace on earth" begins at home!

For centuries men have kept
an appointment with Christmas.
Christmas means fellowship,
feasting, giving and receiving,
a time of good cheer, home.

W.J. RONALD TUCKER

The World's Strangest Christmas Traditions

Many of the Christmas traditions we experience in North America are practiced around the world, with a few variations. Santa Claus becomes Father Christmas in the U.K. and Commonwealth countries; he's Saint Nicholas in Holland; and he becomes the Three Kings in Spain.

Fortunately, there is still room for individuality in non-U.S. traditions—such as south of the border and Europe, where some of the traditional celebrations are, shall we say, unusual.

* * *

In Venezuela, special church services are held every morning from December 16 to December 24, which isn't so unusual—except that people typically roller-skate to these services, filling the streets with skaters. Why? We don't know. Do you really need a reason to roller-skate to church? In some areas, the streets are even blocked off to traffic for safer skating.

Every December 23, the citizens of Oaxaca City, Mexico, gather for a vibrant festival and display of folk art known as the Night of the Radishes. Artisans have five days to transform radishes into elaborate sculptures, from small animals and people to scenes from the Bible or Aztec legends. These sculptures are not for consumption—the radishes are specially cultivated just for the event, saturated with growth-enhancing fertilizer. Cash prizes are awarded for the best and most original radish art—the grand prize is nothing to sneeze at, about twelve hundred U.S. dollars. The evening ends with an extravagant fireworks display.

Oaxacans aren't the only Christmas celebrants who spice up the holidays with vegetables. Two weeks before Christmas, Lebanese children plant chickpeas, beans, wheat grains, and lentils in cotton wool. On Christmas Day, after two weeks of vigilant watering, the sprouts are "harvested" and used to surround the manger in nativity scenes. Okay, this one's more sweet than strange, but definitely different than heading down to the local hobby store to decorate the manger scene.

Yet another tradition involving food supposedly goes all the way back to Germany in the Middle Ages. Known as the Legend of the Pickle—no, this is not a typographical error, nor do we know whether the pickle should be dill or sweet—it is where a family hangs a glass pickle ornament on the Christmas tree. Whoever finds the camouflaged pickle receives an extra gift "from St. Nicholas." The only problem with its German lineage is that no one in Germany has actually heard of it, so we suspect that what started out as a farce has become a popular activity in thousands of households.

Decorating is a big part of most people's Christmas traditions—how many of us can't fathom Christmas without a Christmas tree? In the Ukraine, however, Christmas trees are often decorated with a certain arthropod that we often associate more with Halloween than Christmas.

According to legend, a poor widow with small children was distraught knowing she couldn't afford to decorate the small pine tree outside their house for Christmas. The family awoke on Christmas morning to find that spiders had decorated their tree with webs, and as the sun rose, the light touched the spider's web, turning it to threads of gold and silver. From that day forward, the widow had all she needed. In her memory, Ukrainian Christmas trees are often decorated with plastic spiders and webs for good luck.

The winner of the strange holiday traditions contest, however, has to be the Mari Lwyd phenomenon. The tradition dates back to a Welsh celebration of the end of the darkest winter days. Each year in south Wales, the designated Mari Lwyd holds a horse's skull on a stick and drapes a long horsehair sheet (or *brethyn rhawn*) over his head, cinching it around the skull to create the effect of a walking horse skeleton. The Mari Lwyd then wanders around town with a band of masked revelers, singing songs, playing pranks, and exchanging challenges and insults in rhyme with staged opponents. In some areas, whoever is "given the bite" by the horse's jaws has to pay a small cash fine.

Who knows how these traditions got started, or exactly why they're so popular. What gives a tradition staying power is that it makes us feel close to our friends, family, and neighbors, and makes us feel like we belong to something. So even though it seems a little weird to wear a horse's skull (it's a little weird to even own a horse's skull), people will probably be doing it many years from now. 🌲

Santa around the World

The jolly old elf we know as Santa has many different names in many different countries—he keeps children awake on Christmas Eve all over the world.

- In Belgium and France, he's known as Pere Noel.
- In Brazil, he's Papai Noel.
- In Chile, he's Viejo Pascuero (literally, "Old Man Christmas").
- In China, he's Dun Che Lao Ren (similarly, this translates to "Christmas Old Man").
- In Finland, he's known as Joulupukki.
- In Hawaii, they call him Kanakaloka.
- In Norway, he's called the Julenissen (or "Christmas gnome").
- In Italy, he's called Babbo Natale.
- In Russia, they call him Dead Moroz (or "Grandfather Frost").
- And in the U.K., he's known simply as Father Christmas.

Were it not for the shepherds,
there would have been no reception.
And were it not for a group of stargazers,
there would have been no gifts.

MAX LUCADO

Sharing Christmas

ROBIN MARTENS

"The kids aren't coming home this Christmas," my husband announced abruptly after hanging up the phone. I looked up from reading the paper.

"What do you mean, they're not coming home?" I asked, incredulous. "What is Christmas without family? We've never had Christmas without our kids since they were born."

But it was true—we would be on our own for Christmas. Our daughter was visiting her husband's family in Texas, and our son living in Oregon couldn't get away from work. Our empty nest wasn't too lonely most of the time, but I knew I would really miss them at Christmas. Who was going to eat all the cookies I traditionally baked?

I didn't know how to handle my first empty-nest Christmas. So I was somewhat relieved when a friend emailed me later that week and asked if we would consider hosting two young Korean business men who were coming to study English at the University of Nebraska.

"What do you think?" I asked my husband that evening as we sat together on the couch. I watched cinnamon candles flicker by the fireplace as Gene pondered the decision.

He cleared his throat. "Well, we don't have any big holiday plans, and I'm sure it would be interesting."

It was settled. I got to work fixing up our daughter's old room for guests, feeling a pang of sadness as I plucked her glow-in-the-dark stars from the ceiling.

Young Hock and Lee Song arrived on a rainy night. Over Italian food, we tried to make our new guests feel welcome, although our conversation took a bit of work—their English was very good, but their accents were thick. More than once, I offered a somewhat dishonest nod, hoping I wasn't signifying that I played in a rock band or knew how to hang glide.

Young and Lee had rented a car to drive to school. They had international drivers' licenses, but they needed to learn to drive in Nebraska—quickly. The first time we rode with them, Young drove right through a stop sign. Needless to say, they had different traffic signals in Korea.

Lee and Young were pleasant and cooperative, but had a hard time adjusting to American food. And so they introduced us to kimchi, roasted seaweed, and hot pepper soup. Korean food seemed strange to us at first, but before long we were big fans of kimchi and even started craving it a week later.

The guys told us about their families and their work situations. "In Korea, it isn't unusual for men to work from sunup to sundown because the job situation is so competitive. If you won't work long hours, others are waiting to take your job."

Lee told us, "In Seoul, your house would be worth millions of dollars, because there are so many people and space is limited."

Both Young and Lee worked at prestigious jobs, but lived in small apartments in high-rise buildings. Suddenly our modest suburban home felt like a mansion.

One night we needed more lettuce to make Korean lettuce wraps with rice, bean paste, kimchi, and bacon. Young said with a little chuckle, "If we run out of lettuce in Korea, someone just gets up from the table, goes to the grocery store on another level of our building, and comes back with the food."

As the holiday neared, we shared American Christmas traditions with our guests. We drove them around the neighborhoods to see impressive Christmas lighting displays. As they oohed and aahed, we saw our country's prosperity with new eyes.

Just before Christmas, we invited Lee and Young to help us put up and decorate our tree. We put on a Karen Carpenter Christmas CD—which they loved—and played other Christmas songs that made up a family tradition that went back to when our kids were small, including some Disney carols. Young and Lee threw themselves into the task of decorating, and ornaments and tinsel were rapidly fastened to the branches with a flourish. We had to hurry to keep up with them. When we were finished, we all stepped back to admire our slightly haphazard masterpiece.

"That was wonderful," Lee said.

"Yes," Young replied. "From now on, my family will do this every Christmas."

We sent them back with a few Christmas ornaments to kick-start their new traditions. And I realized, as we waved goodbye, that the Christmas I'd been dreading had been made wonderful as I shared it with strangers from across the globe. Something about the four of us coming together and sharing our different meals, traditions, and lifestyles made this Christmas a holiday to remember.

Say "Merry Christmas" in Fourteen Different Countries!

1. Mexico: "Feliz Navidad"

2. Austria: "Froelich Weinachten"

3. Poland: "Wesolych Swiat"

4. Portugal: "Feliz Natal"

5. Croatia: "Sretan Bozic"

6. The Philippines: "Maligayang Pasko"

7. France: "Joyeux Noël"

8. Italy: "Buone Feste Natalizie"

9. Lithuania: "Linksmu Kaledu"

10. Serbia: "Hristos se rodi"

11. Argentina: "Felices Pasquas"

12. Bulgaria: "Tchestita Koleda"

13. Denmark: "Glædelig Jul"

14. China (Cantonese): "Saint Dan Fai Lok"

An International Christmas Feast

Food is a major component of all holiday celebrations, and very often what you eat around December 25 shows where you're from.

- In Venezuela, the traditional Christmas Eve dinner is *pan de jamón*, a long bread filled with cooked ham and raisins, and *dulce de lechoza*, a dessert made of green papaya and brown sugar.
- Portuguese families eat a meal on Christmas Eve called *Consoada*, consisting of codfish with cabbage and potatoes. For dessert, the feasters might eat *filhoses* or *filhós*, which are made from fried pumpkin dough.
- Traditional after-Mass Mexican dishes include tamales, rice, rellenos, *atole* (a sweet drink), or *menudo*, a drink that some say has a stronger effect than strong coffee.

- In Jamaica, the official holiday feast consists of rice and gungo peas, roast chicken or duck, and oxtails and curried meat.
- The first course of the Danish Christmas feast is a rice porridge with cinnamon and milk. Often a single almond is hidden in the porridge; whoever finds the almond in their bowl receives an extra gift.

Whether you eat one of these treats or an age-old fruitcake, the point of Christmas food is to raise your glass with friends and family and enjoy each other's company. So eat up!

What would the holidays be without food? Lots of food!

Some people panic about waistlines this time of the year. After eating everything they want all year, they suddenly want to go on a diet. Don't give in to the temptation.

Celebrate and enjoy yourself—and remember that food has no calories this week!

The most vivid memories of Christmases
past are usually not of gifts given
or received, but of the spirit of love,
the special warmth of Christmas worship,
the cherished little habits of the home.

LOIS RAND

The Fruitcake Caper

LYDIA E. HARRIS

Fruitcake: You either love it or hate it. Each resident of our large white-with-green-trim farmhouse at the end of Brown Road in Blaine, Washington, loved it. That might have been the problem. My parents, two older brothers, five sisters, and I (the youngest) all yearned for thick slices of fruitcake each Christmas.

It wasn't just any slice of fruitcake we wanted. We didn't crave the heavily brandied cakes in fancy tins from expensive department stores, nor the cheaper cakes made mostly of batter without much candied fruit. No, we longed for Mother's homemade recipe—spicy, fruity, with the crunch of walnuts. Hers was heavy, rich, and dark-colored. Perfect. Once it was cut, each slice revealed shiny jewels of colored citron, begging to be nibbled. Each bite blended candied fruits, plump raisins, and crunchy walnuts mingled with spices and vanilla.

According to tradition, our family started baking fruitcake around Thanksgiving and let it age until Christmas. I helped

Mother measure the ingredients and mix the cake in her large aluminum bread bowl. The batter was a delicious spice cake by itself, and I often sneaked a tasty fingerful. We coated the sticky citron with flour, separating each piece so that the candied peels would mix evenly throughout the cake. When the batter was ready, we lined loaf pans with waxed paper or brown paper bags to keep the delectable cake from sticking (non-stick sprays weren't available then). We made several batches, not only loaf-shaped ones, but also a larger cake baked in an angel food pan. We decorated the tops with candied cherries and walnut halves we had shelled.

As the fruitcake baked, the sweet, spicy aroma wafted through the house, and my mouth watered. I couldn't wait to sample it. We were allowed a small taste but couldn't eat our fill—the fruitcake would be saved for Christmas and rationed to last into the new year. Mother wrapped the cakes in cotton dishtowels and stored them in a large pressure cooker in the pantry to safely age until Christmas.

One December, unbeknownst to anyone else, my oldest brother started making a secret stop by the pantry on his way to work each morning.

On Christmas Day, Mother opened the pressure cooker to remove the prized fruitcake. To her surprise, inside she found only one partially eaten fruitcake and a knife. My brother had cut thick slices for his lunch as he left for work every morning.

We couldn't hold it against him—it was the season of "goodwill toward men," including brothers. Instead, we just laughed that he got away with his fruitcake caper for a whole month.

More than thirty years later, I still bake fruitcake at Thanksgiving, following Mother's prized recipe. My daughter and grandchildren help me mix the batter in the old, now dented, aluminum bread bowl. But we don't store the cake until Christmas; instead, we enjoy it throughout December. We even nibble slices after decorating our Christmas tree. No one needs to sneak a slice.

Even so, to this day I sometimes mail a small loaf of fruitcake and a plastic knife to my brother, now in his seventies, and chuckle as I reminisce about his youthful fruitcake caper.

The Ten Most Delicious Christmas Sweets

1. Sugar cookies
2. Gingerbread—houses or men
3. Fudge
4. Divinity
5. Yule log
6. Kregel
7. Mince pie
8. Peanut butter fudge
9. Eggnog
10. Wassail

Home for the Hollandaise

A man goes into his dentist's office in incredible pain. The dentist examines him briefly and exclaims, "Holy smokes! That metal plate I inserted in your mouth a few months ago is completely corroded. What have you been eating?"

"Well, all I can think of is that my wife made asparagus last month with a special sauce—Hollandaise. I love that stuff—I've been eating it on meat, vegetables, eggs, everything."

His dentist replies, "That's probably it. Hollandaise is made with lots of lemon juice, which is highly acidic and corrosive. I'll have to insert a new plate, but this one will be made out of chrome."

"Why chrome?" the man asks.

"Well, everyone knows there's no plate like chrome for the Hollandaise." 🌲

Green Tea and Chocolate

MARLENE DEPLER

'T was the week before Christmas, and all through the house, I was the only creature stirring. The visions of sugarplums dancing in my wee little head prompted me to eat four milk chocolate truffles before I could even blink an eye, undeterred by the knowledge that these chocolates were supposedly purchased to go into my children's Christmas stockings.

And then, worried that my tummy might indeed turn to a bowl full of jelly, I brewed myself a cup of organic green tea, hoping it would counteract the effects of my aforementioned indulgence—I had once read somewhere that green tea was good for one's health, though I'm still not sure just why.

I sat down with my cup of tea to read the morning paper when what to my wondering eyes should appear...no, not Santa, sleigh, or reindeer, but an article entitled, "Chocolate: The New Health Food?"

I instantly felt better—healthier, more energized, and

decidedly less guilty. I knew there must be a logical explanation for my love affair with smooth, creamy dark chocolate.

The article elaborated on a study that found that those who ate chocolate and candy lived almost a year longer than those who did not, and went on to explain that chocolate contains phenols, which are known to be antioxidants. Even though the scientists cautioned that the findings are preliminary, I am convinced that chocolate is indeed a health food. No doubt in my mind whatsoever.

Now there is no need for clandestine encounters with chocolate. I will openly divulge the secret of my long term relationship with the latest health food. No more justification or rationalization. Furthermore, if I follow my chocolate of choice with a few sips of green tea, the combination of two will undoubtedly lengthen my life even more.

Salud—to long life and lots of antioxidants, including and especially my sweet, velvet-smooth friend, chocolate. Maybe if I leave a cup of green tea alongside Santa's chocolate chip cookies, that will prolong the jolly old elf's career another year.

A Holiday Dieter's Diary

December 1:

I'm cursing the day I decided to begin a diet after Thanksgiving. What was I thinking, anyway? I know it had to do with the New Year's cruise and my need to minimize my poolside jiggling, but that ocean liner feels like a thousand years away right this second—my son just asked if I could bake cookies for his Scout troop party.

December 5:

Found a magazine article on how to avoid holiday overeating. I think maybe I can do this.

December 6:

Tossed the magazine in the fireplace after eating half a batch of sugar cookie dough. I could swear the little dough boy on the package was laughing at me, so he was next.

December 8:

To save calories, I made cabbage soup for dinner tonight, which I chased with a couple of those cherry-flavored candy canes.

December 10:

Tomorrow night's Janie's Christmas party, so I've got to prioritize my hors d'oeuvres—I do love a good cheese ball, but I like those little powdered sugar cookies just a little bit more. Both are equally unhealthy, so maybe I'd just better stick with the cookies. Hey, got to make some sacrifices somewhere.

December 15:

I think I'd have to run about six miles to make up for everything I ate at the office party. Instead, I jumped rope on the linoleum in the kitchen and snagged some of the garland, catapulting it onto the counter and spilling the sprinkles for the cookies. The good news: The ensuing mopping surely burned a few extra calories.

December 16:

I can't back out of making gingerbread cookies with my daughter—it's a tradition. How I'm going to manage not to eat any of the cookies or dough is the problem. Maybe I could have my jaw wired shut between now and this weekend.

December 23:

Haven't lost any weight. But I'm convinced I can turn this thing around. And that's obviously a completely delusional statement, inasmuch as I just went shopping for Christmas dinner, which includes heavy cream in at least three dishes.

December 25:

I have waved the white flag—there was chocolate in my stocking, and I couldn't resist making coffee cake for breakfast. Isn't dieting what January is for, anyway?

A History of Jell-O

You may think you know Jell-O. You know the Jell-O salads, Jell-O cakes, and various other molds and candies that Jell-O brings to the holiday season. What you may not realize is that this Christmas favorite has been around more than one hundred years.

The very first powdered gelatin showed up in 1845, patented by Peter Cooper. In 1897, the patent was sold to a cough syrup mogul named Pearle B. Wait, whose wife came up with the name "Jell-O," and the Waits continued to sell Jell-O in a variety of flavors. The Jell-O formula changed hands a few times, finally settling with the Genesee Pure Foods Company in 1900 (which would later combine with a handful of brands to form the General Foods Corporation, now in association with Kraft Foods, Inc.).

From there, the makers of Jell-O continued to experiment. Cola and apple flavors appeared and disappeared, and the brand expanded into puddings and sugar-free formulas. But through the years, Jell-O has stayed largely the same.

Somewhere along the line, Jell-O became a holiday staple, which only makes sense. It may not be terribly sophisticated, but it's easy and colorful and fun and kid-friendly—all components of a perfect holiday tradition.

*Food doesn't just feed
our bodies—when we gather
together around the table,
food can feed our souls.*

ANONYMOUS

Hot Tamales

It's a Christmas tradition, a staple celebration, in many traditional Hispanic families: tamales. Often made in assembly lines around a kitchen table, holiday tamales might be filled with pork or chicken, beans or fruit, but they're always a symbol of family and tradition.

Tamales are made by spreading masa (a corn-flour dough) on cornhusks, spreading on the filling, and bundling it all together to be cooked in a steamer. The choice of filling might reflect a regional taste, or just a family's favorite. It's a labor-intensive culinary undertaking, but the time is spent talking, laughing, and sharing stories. According to tradition, the finished tamales are eaten after Christmas Eve mass with hot chocolate or for breakfast on Christmas morning. 🌲

Here's a recipe that's sure to be a crowd-pleaser on your next sleigh ride—or as you pile into the van to go look at Christmas lights.

OVEN CARAMEL CORN

15 cups popped unsalted popcorn
$1/2$ cup butter or margarine
1 cup firmly packed brown sugar
$1/4$ cup light corn syrup
$1/2$ teaspoon salt
$1/2$ teaspoon baking soda

Preheat oven to 200°. Divide popcorn between two thirteen-by-nine-inch baking pans; set aside. In a small saucepan over medium heat, combine butter, brown sugar, corn syrup, and salt. Stirring constantly, bring just to a boil. Remove from heat. Stir in baking soda. Slowly pour mixture over popped corn, tossing to coat. Bake one hour, stirring every fifteen minutes. Makes fifteen servings.

*It's a scientific fact
that Christmas cookies
and treats have no calories
between November 20
and December 31.*

GRANDMA'S COOKIE-CUTTER SUGAR COOKIES

CREAM TOGETHER:

$^1/_2$ cup margarine

$^3/_4$ cup sugar

BEAT IN:

1 egg

1 $^1/_2$ teaspoon vanilla

SIFT TOGETHER:

1 $^1/_2$ cup flour

1 teaspoon baking powder

$^1/_4$ teaspoon salt

Mix together and chill in refrigerator for eight hours. Roll on a floured surface; cut with cookie cutter shapes. Bake at 350° for eight to ten minutes, or until edges are barely brown.

The Best Icing:

Mix:

2 $\frac{1}{2}$ cups confectioners' sugar

4 tablespoons melted butter

Beat in:

I egg white

Add:

2-3 tablespoons cream and more sugar until
the icing has a good spreading consistency

Modern culture has been described as the "privacy fence society" in contrast to the seemingly lost "front porch" interaction of another generation.

Christmas is a great time to push outside of your comfort zone and interact with your neighbors, your "village." The thing about the fun and laughter of Christmas is that it's catching—the more time you spend with your friends and neighbors, the more Christmas spirit you'll find you have.

A merry Christmas to everybody!
A happy New Year to all the world!

CHARLES DICKENS

The Christmas Wreath Caper

KATHLEENE S. BAKER

The air was frigid and the sky was gray. Snowflakes drifted gracefully to the ground, which was already hidden beneath a blanket of fluffy white. Sparkling lights shone through windows where Christmas trees held center stage. Bushes and rooftops were twinkling, and wreaths adorned front doors. In this small Kansas town, the holiday spirit was in full swing—even the weather was participating.

Barbara, and her daughter, Gay, had joined in the hustle and bustle that December morning. What better way to get into the spirit of the season than Christmas shopping? They dashed in and out of stores searching for ideal gifts, humming along with Christmas carols in the background. As the snow continued to fall, the two ladies shopped until they nearly dropped.

As they pulled out of the parking lot and onto a busy street, Gay said, "Hey, why don't we drop in on Anna for a cup of tea?

How's that sound?"

"Sounds great! A cup of tea might just perk me up after that shopping marathon."

Without a doubt, Barbara and Gay make up one fun-loving mother and daughter duo. What one doesn't dream up, the other one will, and nothing is off limits when it comes to having a good time. They're basically harmless gals (most of the time); it's just that they're relentless in their search for fun.

Walking up to Anna's front door, Gay remarked, "Oh, look at her beautiful wreath! Look how huge it is, Mom. Wow, I bet she paid a pretty penny for that thing."

While waiting for Anna to answer the door, they oohed and aahed over the wreath hanging at eye level. They rang, pounded, and hollered before deciding no one was home.

They were nearly to the car when Barbara turned and glanced back at the wreath once again. "Isn't that the most beautiful thing you've ever seen?"

"Yep, it's great! I'd kill for one like that. Mom, you can't just stand there gawking at it all day, so let's get going. Come on—it's freezing out here." Gay was brushing snow from the shoulders of her coat and shaking it out of her hair.

Suddenly, Barbara's eyes danced. With a spirited, impish look on her face, she turned to her daughter. "Let's steal it!"

Equally impish laughter exploded on Gay's face as she agreed to the plot.

"But it goes to my house 'cause I don't have my wreath up yet. Besides, Anna will be dropping by in a few days. I can't wait until she lays eyes on it!" quipped Barbara.

Gay dashed back to the house, kicking up snow behind her, and snatched it off its hook, and the wreath-nappers made a clean getaway.

Several days later Anna arrived for tea as expected. Barb took her time getting to the door, and idled by the doorknob for a moment. After several deep breaths, she managed to open it with a straight face, confident in her acting chops. Expecting accusations from Anna, she had to be convincing when she claimed to have purchased the exact same wreath.

"Hi, Barb." Anna was smiling like a Christmas angel, her eyes on the wreath. "You know, I have a wreath almost exactly like that! I thought I'd already hung it, but I noticed a day or so ago it isn't there. I get so confused sometimes, especially this time of year— maybe I just thought I hung it."

Barbara chewed the inside of her cheek, trying not to laugh. "Well, it's new, and when I saw it I just couldn't pass it up. Thanks for the compliment. Now get in here out of the cold. How are you this morning?" Barbara was putting on an award-winning performance.

They chatted, drank tea, and worked on their latest cross-stitch projects. Barbara could only assume Anna was losing her vision, her mind, or both, as there was no more mention of the wreath.

They had a tremendous amount of gossip to catch up on, and by the time Anna was ready to leave, Barbara had completely forgotten about the stolen property adorning her front door.

Walking out, Anna thanked Barb for the enjoyable morning and then suddenly turned around. "I just love your wreath!" Snow crunched with each footstep as Anna walked to her car; she hopped in and waved as she backed out of the driveway. Barbara slowly closed the door behind her, leaned against it, and slid to the floor laughing.

Several days later Anna's phone rang. "Hello?"

"Hi, Anna, it's Barb. I dropped by this morning but you weren't home again. I just keep missing you."

"Sorry about that, I was out running errands. All this last

minute shopping is about to do me in. I don't know if I'm coming or going!"

Barbara took a deep breath and pinched herself to keep from snickering. "When you got home, did you see the wreath on your door?"

There was a short pause. "Well…no. Gee, who's confused now? Remember, I told you I thought I had hung my wreath, but guess I didn't. Every time I think about yours, I plan to get mine out, but I just keep getting sidetracked."

Another pause, and Barb wasn't filling in the silent gaps.

Anna finally let go with a deafening screech, "Oh, don't tell me! You didn't give me your wreath, did you? I know I went on and on about how lovely yours was, but I didn't expect you to give it away. Did you give it to me?"

"No, Anna, I didn't give it to you—but I did return it."

There was another lapse in conversation. "What do you mean, you returned it? You're really confusing me now! My wreath still isn't up—I already told you that. I just thought it was."

The itch of laughter in Barbara's voice finally gave her away as she sputtered, "Think, Anna! Just think—I know you can do it."

Suddenly Barbara heard the squeaking hinges of Anna's front

door as it opened, then the phone crashed to the floor, which startled Barbara something terrible. The last thing she heard was Anna babbling and squealing. It was obvious she had forgotten about her phone now located somewhere on the floor.

Feeling like one of Santa's mischievous elves, Barb gently hung up her phone, did a little jig, and burst into a chorus of "It's Beginning to Look a Lot Like Christmas."

Christmas Groaners

If you find these jokes funny, it's possible that you're an overwhelmed Christmas shopper on the verge of a nervous breakdown. You might want to take a seat.

What do you call a bunch of grandmasters
of chess bragging in a hotel lobby?
Chess nuts roasting in an open foyer.

* * *

Why was Santa's little helper depressed?
Because he had low elf esteem.

* * *

What do you get when you cross
a snowman with a vampire?
Frostbite.

Toy Crazes

You know you're near a toy store at Christmastime if you see grown men and women engaging in full-contact wrestling over a Power Ranger. They even made a movie featuring a certain governor of California as a father intent on securing a TurboMan for his son in *Jingle All the Way*. Remember these toy crazes?

- Tickle Me Elmo (date of craze: Christmas 1996). Like most great ideas, it was a simple one: a doll that laughs when you tickle him. So sweet. So fuzzy. And Sesame Street's preternaturally happy Elmo was the perfect cover for the apparent mind-control device that brought parents out to malls in droves. Rumor has it one parent paid almost $2000 for an Elmo.
- The Cabbage Patch Doll (date of craze: Christmas 1983). Like Elmo, the CPD was sweet and squishy with lots of personality. The smiley, dimple-faced dolls

weren't just bought, they were "adopted," complete with a birth certificate which turned kids into adoptive parents.

- Furby (date of craze: Christmas 1998). A futuristic, interactive ball of fur, the Furby gurgled and sang its way into kids' hearts. It could learn English words, teach Furbish, and generally work kids and adults into a Furby frenzy.

Sociologists may never be able to tell us whether it's parents or kids who go crazier for toys. So we might as well brace ourselves for the next toy trend, be it a stuffed monkey that snowboards or the latest in video game systems. A word to the wise: If you hit the toy stores the day after Thanksgiving, bring your elbow pads.

Manager to department store Santa:
"No 'Ho ho ho' at all, Mr. Reynolds,
is better than a 'Ho ho ho' that
doesn't come from the heart."

AUTHOR UNKNOWN

The Elf and the Christmas Cowboy

GLENN A. HASCALL

"You're going to play an elf," Jack gruffly informed Steve while lighting another cigarette.

"An elf?" asked Steve.

"What? You got wax in your ears? Listen up! An elf—Danny the Elf," Jack barked as he alternated between a coughing fit and fiddling with his handlebar moustache. Then, to amplify his point, he removed his cowboy hat. The Stetson stubbornly released its grip with a sound reminiscent of a cow pulling its hoof from the mud.

Steve certainly had no intention of wearing green tights, let alone curled shoes with bells. Besides that, where did one go to find pointed ears on such short notice? Ah yes, this being radio, Jack was simply after the voice. You see, Steve was cursed with an uncanny ability to impersonate others. Consequently, an elf would probably be easy enough—although he couldn't quite recall ever meeting any elves.

Just months earlier, Jack had taken over as general manager of the small-town radio station where Steve worked, and his pet slogan was "Never say, 'new and improved, just say 'better and better.'" He actually got testy if Steve did anything hinting that he'd forgotten this sacred motto. So on this day our hero was simply asked to "be the elf"—not the new and improved elf, just one that gets better and better.

For this Santa-and-elf bit, children would be sending in letters to the jolly old elf, and Steve and Jack would read them on the air daily after school let out—Jack as Mr. Jolly and Steve as his impish sidekick, Danny, in a bold effort to leave the young listeners with warm childhood memories. Jack would wax eloquent while chain smoking. Steve, on the other hand, would simply listen and respond appropriately.

"Hello, boys and girls, I'm Danny the Elf and I'm really excited today 'cause we have loads of letters to read." Steve was hoping Jack would reply soon—this imitation of an extremely happy, helium-filled gnome was making his head feel a bit like a balloon under pressure. When Jack didn't respond, Steve wheezed, "Isn't that right, Santa?"

"Oh yes, uh, that's right...umm, Denny," Jack paused to puff on that ever-present cigarette.

"You're such a kidder, Santa. Denny is my twin brother in shipping. I'm Danny the radio-sidekick-elf," Steve chuckled in passable elfin tones.

"Right! Sorry, Daren," Jack replied, nonplussed, with a "ho ho ho" that sounded more like "ho ho—" *hack*. "My goodness, we sure do have lots of letters today, and my stars but they're purty. Sort of reminds me of... uh, what was the question?" A rustling of the envelopes followed as Jack tried to find one that was open.

"Tell you what, Santa," Steve interrupted. "Why don't we take a quick little break and check on Comet and Blitzen while the listeners find out more about the Christmas specials at Grommet's Five and Dime?" Steve pressed a button as a pre-recorded seasonal greeting floated across the airwaves. Steve took a moment to check on Jack. "Are you okay?"

"Just fine, Dinky," came Jack's testy reply through the smoky fog.

Steve hopped back in the announcer's chair as the commercial came to an end. "Welcome back. I'm Danny the Elf and I think Santa is next door," he said, careful to leave things open ended for Jack to enter into the conversation.

"That's right, Dwayne. I've just been so impressed with the letters the kids have sent me this year," he paused.

"Wonderful letters," Steve enthused, "marvelous letters."

"Sure! Why take this letter from little Emily, for instance. She's looking for a real live heifer and a fifty-pound bag of seed corn." Jack chuckled with a hearty series of ho's.

"Seed corn and cows, Santa?" Steve asked.

"Oh, sorry, Donny. It seems there's a market report lying on my desk. Santa got a little confused. Oh, but lookie here, Connie is looking for a Radio Flyer and a St. Bernard—say, aren't those dogs the ones with the barrel of... oh, ho ho!" Jack stopped and chuckled nervously in a sort of chortle-fest mixed liberally with a clearing of the throat. Steve briefly considered suggesting a throat lozenge but thought better of it.

Just then, the fire department scanner went off in the next room as staff members suddenly came back to life. They were temporarily incapacitated by what they were hearing from their radios, unsure if it actually qualified as "better and better."

Jack continued to read bits and pieces of letters while encouraging parents to find everything their kids wanted at Grommet's. One of Steve's coworkers sneaked into the control room with a note advising him of the location of the fire. Being that this was a small-town station, Steve was honor bound to air those fire calls whenever they came in. He was sure the audience needed a friendly reminder that emergency vehicles would be careening down the streets shortly and that they should keep an eye out and get their assorted goats and chickens off the roads.

Steve aired the recorded fire announcement, then turned on the microphone to name the location of the blaze, "Well kids, it looks like old man McGowen's barn is going up in flames. Stay in your yards and watch out for the volunteer fire department—and to all a good night."

Suddenly there were several astonished faces looking in at Steve from the outside offices. In that moment he realized he had "been the elf" during the fire call. For the first and last time in station history, a fire call had been handled by an elf.

Considering the guttural sounds emanating from the foggy recording studio, Jack apparently had not thought this a "better and better" moment.

All these years later, us kids beg Grandpa Steve to tell us the story of "The Elf and the Christmas Cowboy," replete with his elfin charm. Every year, the story just gets better and better—and sometimes it even seems new and improved (although we're hoping that Jack never finds out). 🌲

The Blizzard

SUSIE WARREN

We moved to our Denver suburb from West Texas, where we rarely saw a snowflake. So when it started snowing our second December in the Rockies, my husband, two daughters, and I eagerly looked forward to a white Christmas. I'd ordered Christmas stockings for the girls from a lady who lived in our town, custom knit with their names sewn into the hem, and had bought all the trimmings for a perfect Christmas dinner.

But it kept snowing—and then it snowed some more. And before too long, we were in the middle of an all-out blizzard, with snowdrifts billowing above my head.

Obviously, Christmas wasn't going to happen much like I'd envisioned it. With the roads completely packed with snow, we were pretty much stuck in our neighborhood—no light tours, few parties. And I doubted I'd see those perfect stockings before Christmas morning. At least we could still have our Christmas dinner.

But to my surprise, the stockings made their way to me a few days before Christmas—their creator happened to be in the neighborhood. And in the end, I didn't even fix a whole Christmas dinner. Several families on our street gathered at a neighbor's house to eat, sing carols, and just talk.

We may have been snowed in, but there was plenty of warmth between neighbors that Christmas.

A Modern Look at A Christmas Carol:
A Journaling Activity for Advanced Composition

MRS. KREEGLE, 5TH HOUR
Caroline Ashley

DECEMBER 13

It is so Friday the Thirteenth. We've got to read this ancient book by some old guy named William Dickerson. Or something like that. He's English, I think. I think he wrote Romeo and Juliet and some other musicals. The book's not that long but oh my gosh, you should try to read how this guy writes. I thought the book had pictures but it's absolutely all words.

We have to write in this journal while we read the book. I haven't actually started the book yet. I called Tracy and Rachel. They don't know if the movie is just like the book or not. So I might have to actually read this.

DECEMBER 16

I am so far behind. No way was I going to write this weekend. I mean, it's Christmas, right? I had to go shopping and stuff. You know, get in the spirit.

I have started reading. This old dude, Ebinasher Scudge, who is like five times older than my grandma, is so mean. All he cares about is money. I don't think there's anything wrong with that part because a lot of money is a good thing. My problem is I never have enough. My dad only gives me like $25 a week!!! Can you believe that? Sometimes I even have to pay for movies and stuff. Usually my mom will give me a few extra bucks, though. If I have to apply this to modern life, I guess my dad can be like that Ebiscrudger Sneeze guy.

DECEMBER 17

Two nights in a row of the Christmas book. I've got to rent the movie. I'm so tired but no way was I going to miss "American Idol." Brandon is so hot.

Anyway, that Scroone dude wasn't hot. He kept his
offices real cold and the guy who worked for him,
Bob Hatchet, got cold sometimes. Scroone got mad
at him when he put extra coal in the fireplace. Coal
in the fireplace?! I think maybe that Hatchet guy
should have got yelled at. Coal like messes up the
environment. Dad wouldn't drive me to the mall on
Sunday. He said we don't need to go shopping on a
church day and besides gas prices were so high we
needed to drive less. I guess he's a lot like Scroone.

DECEMBER 19

No way was I going to read last night. Mrs.
Kreegle let us read in class and then Tracy and Rachel
and me went to Starbucks after school and got
caramel frappuccinos and talked to a couple guys
from the basketball team that we know and then did
some more reading.

I thought the ghost part was going to be good.
You know, real scary! But the ghost dude,

Morbey, was an old dude too! He like shook some chains or something. But it's not like I had to close my eyes or anything. Ha ha! It's a book with no pictures. Guess I'd never have to close my eyes. I'm going to call Tracy and Rachel and tell them my joke.

I am so confused now. I don't know if that Sponge dude died or got married or what! I guess he has a girlfriend but he sounds so gross. My grandpa has lots of hair on his ears and in his nose. I bet Sponge was just like him. The author, Sheldon Shakeinson, is kind of confusing. I bet if he was a writer today he'd be like on the sale table at Barnes and Noble. Like $2 for a big hardcover book. I don't know if anybody buys them anyway. I wouldn't!

DECEMBER 20

Oh man, I was supposed to finish the book last night and turn it in today. No way Mrs. Kreegle is going to read it over the weekend anyway. So I got up at five this morning. Unbelievable. Starbucks doesn't open until six. Dad promised to take me as soon as they opened. He never even knocked on the bathroom door to let me know what time it is. So it was like 6:30 before I got there. He was in such a bad mood. Just like Mr. Scrubber or that ghost dude.

I have to skip ahead. Scrubber got like real happy. He was like freaking people out. He bought a turkey from some guy on the street. I'm not sure I believe that part. It's not realistic. Who has a turkey walking down the street?

He went over to that Hatchet guy's house. He had a little kid living in his house named Tiny Tim. I saw this special on TV once and I thought Tiny Tim was like this big gross old dude who has a real high voice. I couldn't help thinking about him when I was reading the last couple pages. That Hatchet guy had to be really strong to carry Tiny

Tim out to the kitchen. Ha ha! Tracy and Rachel are going to crack up. I'll bet they like get in trouble with Mrs. Kreegle because they can't stop laughing. Rachel said no way is Mrs. Kreegle actually going to read this. She better be right or I am so in trouble. But how can Mrs. Kreegle grade this down? I'm doing the assignment. I didn't skip that many pages.

My dad is sitting over there reading "The New York Times" and giving me dirty looks and looking at his watch. He says I need to learn the meaning of Christmas. Yeah, I bet Scrudge or whatever that guy's name is was always yelling at Hatchet to hurry up.

I guess Scrudge bought a bunch of presents for Little Timmy and everybody. Okay, my dad's like that too. See, I've got the Christmas spirit! 🌲

Hopefully church is a big part of your life and a source of ho! ho! ho! all year long.

If it isn't, the holidays are a wonderful time to find the comfort of an "old friend"—and rediscover the place where you probably first heard the meaning of Christmas.

And when you see children in bathrobes lift their voice in song—you'll wonder how you ever got away from a place so special.

The trouble with life
is that it's often terribly funny
exactly when it's supposed
to be terribly serious.

ANONYMOUS

Tootin' in the Pews

David Michael Smith

There's something special about the unique and celebratory sounds of a brass ensemble in a two-hundred-year-old church on Christmas Eve night. The mixture of mellow sax and bold brass can both inspire and calm. And when you add the ambiance of candlelight, crimson and ivory poinsettias, and hanging green firs with red berries and holly, you have a holiday setting straight out of heaven itself.

The year was 1973. I was in my final year of junior high school that winter, and a member of the very successful and regionally acclaimed Sussex Central Junior High School marching band. I played tenor saxophone. Comprised of students from two local towns smaller than the map blips they used to salute on *Hee Haw*, we somehow annually formed a band of close to 150 dedicated members, musicians, flag bearers, honor guard, and drum majorette included. And when Sussex entered a parade, we entered to win, second place an insult, first place an expectation.

We were, according to the overflowing trophy cabinet at school, accomplished musicians and marchers, skilled artists, the envy of other school districts.

For Christmas, a few fellow members and I decided that it would be a fun idea to play our instruments at the Christmas Eve midnight mass at St. Paul's Episcopal Church in little Georgetown, Delaware—to give back to our adoring community, the folks that supported us all year long. We envisioned ourselves as saintly heroes, pious purveyors of musical excellence. Our pastor immediately agreed to the proposition, probably because two of the members were his very own sons. I was sure we would be the toast of the congregation that December, our beautiful music sure to make everyone's Christmas just a bit merrier.

We practiced with masterful precision at least once a week, sometimes twice. We planned to perform three songs, to be intermittently played with the choir's vocal concert. The ensemble chose "It Came Upon a Midnight Clear," "Away in the Manger," and for our rousing finale, "God Rest Ye Merry Gentlemen." I had visions of people dancing in the aisles.

Christmas Eve arrived, and we were dressed to the nines for our big Christmas showcase. Every hair was in place. I even polished my sax with my mother's lemon Pledge.

Things went smoothly during our first two songs, and the choir seemed to hook onto our momentum as they sang beautifully. Then it was time for our final carol, and the congregation waited with bated breath.

The church was packed to the rafters, the men in suits and ties, some with holiday images plastered across the brilliant silk, while the ladies wore black or red velvet dresses adorned with gold necklaces and earrings. The building, as if on cue, settled into quietness bred from anticipation and utter excitement. After all, it was Christmas, the greatest time of the year.

Eight sets of eyes eagerly peered at our leader. I licked my moist reed, ready to attack the initial notes of "God Rest Ye Merry Gentlemen." Then, like a symphony conductor at Carnegie Hall, she brought her hands downward in a circular motion and we played.

The first few bars went quite well. The world-famous Canadian Brass Ensemble would've been envious. Crisp, enunciated notes flowed from our instruments, filling the church's hallowed bowels. But then *it* happened.

To this day, I'm still not sure if the sound I heard was what I thought I heard. A prosecuting attorney could've made a convincing case based on the auditory evidence, but at least two other explanations existed, alibis any defense attorney worth his weight in litigation fees would have proposed. At the time of the incident, however, being a teen keen to mischief, I of course assumed the obvious.

With absolute, precise and perfect timing at the end of the third line of music, ironically right after "To save us all from Satan's power, When we were gone astray," and even more coincidental, a breath of air prior to, "O tidings of comfort and joy," a broken, bass-like tone reverberated from my left, where the French horn and trombonist sat. At first I thought it was a sick note, an error from the lips of one of the young students of brass. But the noise had a strange familiarity, one recognized from the boy's locker room or on the homeward-bound school bus, but seldom if ever heard in God's reverent house.

A rapid glance revealed the guilty party: The trombonist, the eldest of the pastor's sons, was red faced and giggling with embarrassment. In an instant, the trumpeter and alto saxophonist were also silently laughing, eyes wet with tears, no longer able to continue the tune. In a flash the entire ensemble was battling laughter that could not be suppressed. Our mirth was like the ocean at high tide: There wasn't a thing that could be done to deny the inevitable. And the more we each eyed the other, the more we became slaves to our master named laughter.

Of course we were in church, surrounded by over a hundred parishioners and visitors and distinguished guests that included the mayor and his wife, in sudden silence, each of us desperately trying to mask the incident by continuing to play and pretend the whole thing never happened. But to properly blow a trumpet, form a note on the smooth, curved mouthpiece of the sax, or direct the right amount of air over the impish hole of the flute requires precision and control, something none of us had.

The French horn suddenly played the next line of the song, alone. In fact, the studious, chubby-cheeked kid behind the French horn masterfully finished the rest of the song by himself, a solo, a one-man concert of sorts, something he had probably always dreamed about. But it was Christmas and dreams sometimes come true on this blessed holiday.

It actually sounded very nice, so I was told later. I earnestly don't recall much about that night—I was too busy gagging on laughter, tickled and shaking with silly and childish glee.

Strangely, we were never invited to play our instruments in church ever again after that night. Thirty years later, I still smile when I hear "God Rest Ye Merry Gentleman" on the radio or at the mall while shopping for Christmas gifts.

I sometimes wonder if what we did was wrong, unpardonable. And then I think of our Lord and believe the Son of God laughed, too, sitting around a campfire with the disciples, sharing stories and anecdotes, laughing until they cried.

Why is it the things that embarrass us the most are also often the very same things that cause us to laugh until our sides ache? I can only hope my Lord heard my prayers for forgiveness that evening at the Communion railing, for my comrades and myself. And I hope that maybe, just maybe, the God of all gods also chuckled and grinned that night at His imperfect children. After all, our intentions were good—nothing was premeditated.

But then again, I never confirmed that with the trombonist.

The Legend of the Poinsettia

They're a staple in holiday decorating schemes—you see the bright red flowers at banks, grocery stores, and especially churches. But how exactly did the poinsettia come to be associated with Christmas?

According to legend, a poor girl in Mexico named Pepita was walking to Christmas Eve services with her cousin Pedro, sad that she had no gift to give the Christ Child. Pedro comforted her, "Even the most humble gift, if given in love, will be acceptable in His eyes."

So Pepita, wanting to give something, even if something small, knelt down beside the road and gathered a bouquet of ordinary weeds. But when she arrived at the church, her sadness returned as she realized just how humble her weed bouquet was.

Remembering Pedro's comforting words, she gently laid the bouquet by the nativity scene. And suddenly, the weeds transformed, blooming into brilliant red flowers. All the worshippers were sure they had seen a Christmas miracle. From that day on, the bright red flowers were called the "Flores de Noche Buena," or "Flowers of the Holy Night," for they returned each year around Christmastime.

Christmas is the gentlest, loveliest
festival of the revolving year—and
yet, for all that, when it speaks,
its voice has strong authority.

W. J. CAMERON

The Four Stages of Life:

1. *You believe in Santa Claus.*
2. *You don't believe in Santa Claus.*
3. *You are Santa Claus.*
4. *You look like Santa Claus.*

AUTHOR UNKNOWN

How to Stay Awake at Midnight Mass

PAUL M. MILLER

Maybe I'm being petty, but if I had to describe the most difficult part of this glorious holiday, it would be what the title of this essay indicates—going to a church where the Christmas Eve service begins at 11:00 P.M. and continues until after midnight.

Catholic kids have lived with this all of their lives. Some of my friends go to Christmas Eve service early in the evening—like at 6:30 or 7:00. But the church my family attends is of the late-night frame of mind, so that puts us in the eleven-to-midnight time slot.

And so, as promised, here is my tried and true list of ways to stay awake during Christmas Eve midnight service.

1. Whatever you do, don't allow yourself to get too comfortable. A lot of church builders must have been pretty smart—their pews are usually hard and straight-backed,

making them very difficult to sleep on. Although I've been in some churches where the pews are padded like a sofa, which is just not helpful at all around 11:45 at night.

2. During the singing, really belt out the songs. It'll get your blood circulating. If you have to yawn in the middle of one, just yawn away—nobody will know the difference.

3. Read all the scriptures and liturgy verbiage with gusto. Such activity is sure to keep you focused. Don't shut your eyes during the Lord's Prayer. Rookie mistake.

4. If your pastor wears a robe or vestments, use your imagination and guess what he has on underneath. Depending on how well you know him, ask him when you shake his hand after service. Remember, this is not a "briefs or boxers" question.

5. If your minister wears a tie, pick out a color from his tie and see how many people in the sanctuary are wearing that same color.

6. Count the number of potted poinsettias, candles, people, windows, doors, men wearing ties, women with hats on, new toys, pews on either side of the aisle, bald-headed men (or women, if you can tell—they're usually pretty secretive about it), that kind of thing.

7. Play with the numbers on the hymn or attendance board, by adding and subtracting the columns of figures. You might also attempt to figure square roots, though I never could do it. I was out of school with a hernia operation when we learned that math. I really doubt if it makes much difference in my career goals to play pro ball.

8. During the sermon listen closely for a certain word and keep track of how many times your minister uses that word. Obviously, "the" won't work, but you might choose something like "human" or "spirit" or "today." My pastor says "uh" quite often, so that's a good one for me.

Don't be too hard on yourself if you fall asleep—it happens to the best of us. Just be careful that no one "sees you when you're sleeping."

Silent Night

The organ of a small church in Arndorf, Austria, had fallen into disrepair. The parish priest, Father Josef Mohr, was troubled that his poor congregation had no money for repairs—and the Christmas season was at hand.

On the day before Christmas Eve, as he trudged home from visiting a family that had lost a loved one, he was awe-struck by the beauty of the surrounding mountains and his peaceful village in the valley below. When he arrived home, he quickly penned the words to a poem inspired by the moment.

He read his poem to a musician, Franz Gruber, the next day. Gruber was so captivated by the words that he wrote a melody to be played on his guitar.

Silent Night was premiered on Christmas morning in 1818 and has been sung by millions in the centuries that have followed. 🌲

It is good to be a child sometimes,
and never better than at Christmas, when
its mighty Founder was a child himself.

CHARLES DICKENS

Room in the Inn

TEENA M. STEWART

"I got something special at the store when I was Christmas shopping," said Janis that night at supper.

Matt and Chloe's eyes brightened and Janis's husband, Mark, raised his eyebrows.

"What is it? What is it?" asked six-year-old Matt, jumping up and down in excitement as he and Chloe followed their mother over to a bag in the corner.

Chloe, the quiet one, said little, but her wide eyes told Janis she was just as excited and curious as Matt. Janis set a brown box on the table, a serial number stamped on the lid in dark black ink. Next to it was a word that Matt couldn't decipher.

"What's that word?" asked Matt.

Janis caught Mark's eye. "You'll understand it after you open the box."

Matt tore through the heavy tape on the box and lifted the lid. The straw-like packing looked like a giant bird's nest.

"Careful," said Janis, helping Chloe and Matt pull out the contents.

Matt pulled out a camel figurine, and then a shepherd. He handed each piece to Chloe who reverently set them on the table. "It's a manger scene."

"Man-jer," said Chloe.

"I saw it today when I was Christmas shopping. There I was with my cart overflowing with Christmas presents and I'm saying to myself, 'Just stay focused. Pay for it and get out.' And then I saw it. I couldn't resist."

She looked at Mark. "Funny how your memory plays hide-and-seek. I had forgotten about the nativity set we'd had as a kid. And then I saw this and it looked so much like it—not one of those sophisticated, bisque porcelain sets, but the old fashioned kind, like I had when I was growing up. I had to get it."

Chloe cherished anything miniature, dolls especially. She had an assortment of small babies given to her by friends and relatives. Here was a delightful grouping of animals and people, even a mother and father. They captivated her. Most wonderful of all was the tiny baby.

As they arranged the set on the end table in the living room,

Chloe could not keep from touching the figures. "No, Chloe. Those are not toys. They're for decoration." Janis caught herself on the word 'decoration' and explained further. "The manger scene is to remind us of the Christmas story."

Even though the children had heard the Christmas story in church, Janis and Mark explained the story again. As usual, Matt was full of questions. Chloe listened with usual, wide-eyed wonder. When Mark got the part where Mary and Joseph needed a place to stay but found no room in the inn, Chloe spoke up.

"They didn't have a place to stay?"

"It worked out okay, Chloe," said Mark. "They ended up staying in the stable. Baby Jesus was born there, surrounded by all the animals. His bed was a manger, something the cows eat from."

Chloe nodded as if she understood.

That night as Janis and Mark prepared for bed, Janis walked past the manger scene.

"Oh no!" she exclaimed.

"What's wrong?" asked Mark.

"Baby Jesus is missing. He must have fallen out of the manger," she said looking around the other figures on the table.

"Maybe someone bumped into it and it fell out," said Mark.

They dropped to the floor and searched but found nothing but a gooey sucker covered with dust bunnies.

"I don't understand," said Janis. "Where could it have gone? What good is a manger scene without a Baby Jesus?"

"Well, maybe He's about his Father's business," said Mark, laughing. Janis shot him a look that said, *Not funny*.

"Don't worry about it. It'll turn up." Mark laid a reassuring hand on her shoulder. "Let's go check on the kids."

The soft sounds of peaceful slumber filled Chloe's bedroom. Her pale face, surrounded by ringlets of dark, curly hair, made her look like part child, part angel.

As Janis leaned over the pillow to give her daughter a kiss, she froze, then lifted her hand to her mouth. She turned toward Mark, her face catching the light from the hallway. Her eyes shimmered with amusement. "You've got to see this," she whispered, motioning him over.

Chloe's small fist lay tightly closed on her pillow. Nestled snugly inside was Baby Jesus, wrapped in doll's tiny blanket, fast asleep. 🌲

Saint Francis and the Christmas Crèche

We've all seen nativity scenes—live ones on church lawns and light-up ones on rooftops. But how did the nativity scene get its start?

The Christmas Crèche has been traced back to St. Francis of Assisi. Legend has it that a few years before he died, St. Francis, a deacon, was visiting the town of Grecio for Christmas and felt moved to celebrate the Nativity in a special way.

Because the Franciscan chapel was too small for the congregation to hold midnight mass there, St. Francis set up an altar in an alcove of rock near the town square. There he commemorated the first Christmas Eve by arranging a manger, some hay for a bed, and an ox and donkey. When the people arrived for mass, they sang psalms and listened to the homily preached by St. Francis. And then, a man named John who had befriended St. Francis during his visit declared that he could see the Babe lying in the manger. Later, several miracles were reported—the congregants testified that the hay they took from the Crèche to their cattle cured all the diseases of the animals.

Since then, the Christmas Crèche has been a popular way to commemorate and celebrate the birth of a Baby.

After
Christmas

All good things must come to an end! Or do they?

Let the laughter and love you've experienced over

Christmas extend to every day of your upcoming year!

'Twas the Bills After Christmas

ADAPTED BY PAUL M. MILLER

'Twas the day after Christmas, and all through the house,
Every creature was hurtin', even the mouse.
The toys were battered, their batteries dead;
Santa's passed out, with some ice on his head.

Wrappings and ribbons still covered the floor,
While upstairs the family continued to snore.
While I in my T-shirt, new kicks, and jeans,
Went down to the kitchen and started to clean.

When out in the yard there arose such a clatter,
I sprang from the sink to see what was the matter.
Away to the back door I flew like a flash.
Tripped over the trashcan, kicked the screen with a crash.

When what to my drooping blue eyes should appear,

But a red, white, and blue truck, with a dent in its rear.
The driver was smiling, so lively and grand;
The patch on his jacket said, "U.S. Post Man."

The handful of bills made him grin like a fox;
While he pulled down the door of our cheery mailbox.
Bill upon bill was tossed in like a game;
And he sniggered and guffawed when he called out their name.

"There's Dillards and Macy's, and Penney's, and Sears,
With Target and Levitz—" I exploded in tears.
"To the top of your limit, in every store, every mall,
 You charged away, charged away, charged away all!"

He whooped and he whistled, as he finished his work.
He filled up our mailbox, then turned with a jerk.
And sprang to his truck, then he drove down the road,
Moving much faster with just half a load.

Then I heard him call out with great holiday cheer,
"Enjoy what you got—you'll be paying all year!"

Christmas is the season
for kindling the fire
of hospitality in the hall,
the genial flame of charity
in the heart.

WASHINGTON IRVING

The Gift That Keeps on Giving

Many shelters and rescue missions report that there are too many volunteers over the holiday season—but not enough at other times of the year. Call a local compassionate ministry and make plans now to help in June or another month. Be sure to mark it on your calendar!

The Pros and Cons of Making New Year's Resolutions

PRO

- It's a good thing to choose to eat more healthy foods and cut back on unhealthy foods.

- Making the decision to get on a regular exercise program is a positive, life-affirming lifestyle issue.

- Revamping your finances is a great move—we begin where we are.

- Getting things organized around the house will decrease your stress and make life run much more smoothly.

- Making resolutions, like goal setting, helps set a positive course of action.

Con

- The only reason you're swearing never to eat sugar again is that you've had eggnog every day for three straight weeks and are literally sick.

- The last time you joined a health club, the elliptical machine kept beeping an alarm for "excess weight."

- There's no worse time for belt-tightening than right after your December credit card statement arrives.

- That professional organizer's business card is buried in your office under some clothes you meant to take to the donation center, the dog's leash, last year's tax returns, and a stack of storage bins (that you bought in order to get organized).

- Resolving not to make any more resolutions doesn't really count as a resolution.

When Should You Take the Decorations Down?

THE PROCRASTINATOR Tomorrow!

THE SCORE KEEPER If I'm going to spend the whole day after Thanksgiving putting these things up while my wife goes shopping, they aren't coming down until February.

THE ACCOUNTANT Utility bills are up 17%—they come down at 12:01 A.M. on December 26.

THE PREOCCUPIED Oh man, I knew I was forgetting to do something this year. I never even put them up.

THE ENTHUSIAST But lights are so pretty any time of the year. I'm leaving mine up until Memorial Day.

THE SECURITY SPECIALIST But lights are such a good crime deterrent any time of year. I'm leaving mine up until Memorial Day.

THE REAL ESTATE AGENT They're charming and nostalgic—leave 'em up until June.

THE GARAGE MUSICIAN If we're the only house in the neighborhood with lights on, that just increases the chances that people will notice our house, which will increase the chances that someone will hear my band play. I say they stay on year-round.

THE SPORTS FAN At halftime, unless the score is tied.

THE FAMILY THERAPIST Lights and other holiday traditions make children feel secure and connected. You can't have too much of a good thing—let's leave them up all year... Now, honey, it makes me feel concerned when I see you ripping the plug out of the outlet.

Acknowledgments

"Angel with an Accent" © Beverly Bush Smith. Used by permission. All rights reserved.

"The Blizzard" © Jessica Inman. Used by permission. All rights reserved.

"Christmas at the Airport" © Patricia Lorenz. Used by permission. All rights reserved.

"Christmas Cookies" © Jo Haring. Used by permission. All rights reserved.

"The Christmas Tree" © Sarah Oliver. Used by permission. All rights reserved.

"The Christmas Wreath Caper" © Kathleene S. Baker. Used by permission. All rights reserved.

"The Elf and the Christmas Cowboy" © Glenn A. Hascall. Used by permission. All rights reserved.

"The Fruitcake Caper" © Lydia E. Harris. Used by permission. All rights reserved.

"Green Tea and Chocolate" © Marlene Depler. Used by permission. All rights reserved.

"How to Give a Spectacular Christmas Gift" © Susan A. Karas. Used by permission. All rights reserved.

"How to Stay Awake at Midnight Mass" © Paul M. Miller. Used by permission. All rights reserved.

"My Newlywed Christmas" © Joan Clayton. Used by permission. All rights reserved.

"My Very Own Santa" © Kathleene S. Baker. Used by permission. All rights reserved.

"The Mystery of the Fruitcake" © Jan Ledford. Used by permission. All rights reserved.

"On the Tradition of Sending Christmas Cards" © Paul M. Miller. Used by permission. All rights reserved.

"The Perfect Gift" © Linda Rondeau. Used by permission. All rights reserved.

"The Purple Stocking" © Karen Robbins. Used by permission. All rights reserved.

"Room in the Inn" © Teena M. Stewart. Used by permission. All rights reserved.

"Rudolph's Sad Demise" © Teena M. Stewart. Used by permission. All rights reserved.

"Santa Sighting" © Lanita Bradley Boyd. Used by permission. All rights reserved.

"Scrambled Christmas" © Darla Satterfield Davis. Used by permission. All rights reserved.

"Sharing Christmas" © Robin Martens. Used by permission. All rights reserved.

"The Spirit of Christmas Past" © Georgia Richardson. Used by permission. All rights reserved.

"Tootin' in the Pews" © David Michael Smith. Used by permission. All rights reserved.

"Twas the Bills after Christmas" © Paul M. Miller. Used by permission. All rights reserved.

"Where Did Prince Charming Go?" © Linda Rondeau. Used by permission. All rights reserved.

"A White Christmas" © Diane Dean White. Used by permission. All rights reserved.

"Who Says Traditions Have to Make Sense" © Jessica Inman. Used by permission. All rights reserved.

"You Bet Your Boots" © Nancy B. Gibbs. Used by permission. All rights reserved.